Boston Red Sox 2020

A Baseball Companion

Edited by R.J. Anderson, Craig Goldstein and Bret Sayre

Baseball Prospectus

Craig Brown, Steven Goldman and David Pease, Consultant Editors
Robert Au, Harry Pavlidis and Amy Pircher, Statistics Editors

Copyright © 2020 by DIY Baseball, LLC.
All rights reserved

This book or any part thereof may not be reproduced or transmitted in any form or by any means, electronic or mechanical, including photocopying, recording, or by any information storage and retrieval system, without permission in writing from the publisher.

Limit of Liability/Disclaimer of Warranty: While the publisher and the author have used their best efforts in preparing this book, they make no representations or warranties with respect to the accuracy or completeness of the contents of this book and specifically disclaim any implied warranties of merchantability or fitness for a particular purpose. No warranty may be created or extended by sales representatives or written sales materials. The advice and strategies contained herein may not be suitable for your situation. You should consult with a professional where appropriate. Neither the publisher nor the author shall be liable for any loss of profit or any other commercial damages, including but not limited to special, incidental, consequential, or other damages.

Library of Congress Cataloging-in-Publication Data:
paperback
ISBN-13: 978-1-949332-66-7

Project Credits
Cover Design: Michael Byzewski at Aesthetic Apparatus
Interior Design and Production: Jeff Pease, Dave Pease
Layout: Jeff Pease, Dave Pease

Baseball icon courtesy of Uberux, from https://www.shareicon.net/author/uberux

Ballpark diagram courtesy of Lou Spirito/THIRTY81 Project, https://thirty81project.com/

Manufactured in the United States of America
10 9 8 7 6 5 4 3 2 1

Table of Contents

Statistical Introduction v

Part 1: Team Analysis

Boston Red Sox: Where Are You Going, Where Have You Been? 3
   Scott Orgera, Alexis Collins and Matthew Trueblood

Performance Graphs 9

2019 Team Performance 10

2020 Team Projections 11

Team Personnel 12

Fenway Park Stats 13

Red Sox Team Analysis 15

Part 2: Player Analysis

Red Sox Player Analysis 22

Red Sox Prospects 107

Part 3: Featured Articles

The Baseball Is Juiced (Again) 125
   Robert Arthur

The Moral Hazard of Playing It Safe 129
   Craig Goldstein

Index of Names 135

Statistical Introduction

Sports are, fundamentally, a blend of athletic endeavor and storytelling. Baseball, like any other sport, tells its stories in so many ways: in the arc of a game from the stands or a season from the box scores, in photos, or even in numbers. At Baseball Prospectus, we understand that statistics don't replace observation or any of baseball's stories, but complement everything else that makes the game so much fun.

What stats help us with is with patterns and precision, variance and value. This book can help you learn things you may not see from watching a game or hundred, whether it's the path of a career over time or the breadth of the entire MLB. We'd also never ask you to choose between our numbers and the experience of viewing a game from the cheap seats or the comfort of your home; our publication combines running the numbers with observations and wisdom from some of the brightest minds we can find. But if you *do* want to learn more about the numbers beyond what's on the backs of player jerseys, let us help explain.

Offense

We've revised our methodology for determining batting value. Long-time readers of the book will notice that we've retired True Average in favor of a new metric: Deserved Runs Created Plus (DRC+). Developed by Jonathan Judge and our stats team, this statistic measures everything a player does at the plate–reaching base, hitting for power, making outs, and moving runners over–and puts it on a scale where 100 equals league-average performance. A DRC+ of 150 is terrific, a DRC+ of 100 is average and a DRC+ of 75 means you better be an excellent defender.

DRC+ also does a better job than any of our previous metrics in taking contextual factors into account. The model adjusts for how the park affects performance, but also for things like the talent of the opposing pitcher, value of different types of batted-ball events, league, temperature and other factors. It's able to describe a player's expected offensive contribution than any other statistic we've found over the years, and also does a better job of predicting future performance as well.

There's a lot more to DRC+'s story, and you can read all about it in greater depth near the end of this book.

The other aspect of run-scoring is baserunning, which we quantify using Baserunning Runs. BRR not only records the value of stolen bases (or getting caught in the act), but also accounts for all the stuff that doesn't show up on the back of a baseball card: a runner's ability to go first to third on a single, or advance on a fly ball.

Defense

Where offensive value is *relatively* easy to identify and understand, defensive value is…not. Over the past dozen years, the sabermetric community has focused mostly on stats based on zone data: a real-live human person records the type of batted ball and estimated landing location, and models are created that give expected outs. From there, you can compare fielders' actual outs to those expected ones. Simple, right?

Unfortunately, zone data has two major issues. First, zone data is recorded by commercial data providers who keep the raw data private unless you pay for it. (All the statistics we build in this book and on our website use public data as inputs.) That hurts our ability to test assumptions or duplicate results. Second, over the years it has become apparent that there's quite a bit of "noise" in zone-based fielding analysis. Sometimes the conclusions drawn from zone data don't hold up to scrutiny, and sometimes the different data provided by different providers don't look anything alike, giving wildly different results. Sometimes the hard-working professional stringers or scorers might unknowingly inflict unconscious bias into the mix: for example good fielders will often be credited with more expected outs despite the data, and ballparks with high press boxes tend to score more line drives than ones with a lower press box.

Enter our Fielding Runs Above Average (FRAA). For most positions, FRAA is built from play-by-play data, which allows us to avoid the subjectivity found in many other fielding metrics. The idea is this: count how many fielding plays are made by a given player and compare that to expected plays for an average fielder at their position (based on pitcher ground ball tendencies and batter handedness). Then we adjust for park and base-out situations.

When it comes to catchers, our methodology is a little different thanks to the laundry list of responsibilities they're tasked with beyond just, well, catching and throwing the ball. By now you've probably heard about "framing" or the art of making umpires more likely to call balls outside the strike zone for strikes. To put this into one tidy number, we incorporate pitch tracking data (for the years it exists) and adjust for important factors like pitcher, umpire, batter and home-field advantage using a mixed-model approach. This grants us a number for how many strikes the catcher is personally adding to (or subtracting from) his pitchers' performance…which we then convert to runs added or lost using linear weights.

Framing is one of the biggest parts of determining catcher value, but we also take into account blocking balls from going past, whether a scorer deems it a passed ball or a wild pitch. We use a similar approach—one that really benefits from the pitch tracking data that tells us what ends up in the dirt and what doesn't. We also include a catcher's ability to prevent stolen bases and how well they field balls in play, and *finally* we come up with our FRAA for catchers.

Pitching

Both pitching and fielding make up the half of baseball that isn't run scoring: run prevention. Separating pitching from fielding is a tough task, and most recent pitching analysis has branched off from Voros McCracken's famous (and controversial) statement, "There is little if any difference among major-league pitchers in their ability to prevent hits on balls hit in the field of play." The research of the analytic community has validated this to some extent, and there are a host of "defense-independent" pitching measures that have been developed to try and extract the effect of the defense behind a hurler from the pitcher's work.

Our solution to this quandary is Deserved Run Average (DRA), our core pitching metric. DRA looks like earned run average (ERA), the tried-and-true pitching stat you've seen on every baseball broadcast or box score from the past century, but it's very different. To start, DRA takes an event-by-event look at what the pitchers does, and adjusts the value of that event based on different environmental factors like park, batter, catcher, umpire, base-out situation, run differential, inning, defense, home field advantage, pitcher role and temperature. That mixed model gives us a pitcher's expected contribution, similar to what we do for our DRC+ model for hitters and FRAA model for catchers. (Oh, and we also consider the pitcher's effect on basestealing and on balls getting past the catcher.)

It's important to note that DRA is set to the scale of runs allowed per nine innings (RA9) instead of ERA, which makes DRA's scale slightly higher than ERA's. The reason for this is because ERA tends to overrate three types of pitchers:

1. Pitchers who play in parks where scorers hand out more errors. Official scorers differ significantly in the frequency at which they assign errors to fielders.
2. Ground-ball pitchers, because a substantial proportion of errors occur on groundballs.
3. Pitchers who aren't very good. Better pitchers often allow fewer unearned runs than bad pitchers, because good pitchers tend to find ways to get out of jams.

Since the last time you picked up an edition of this book, we've also made a few minor changes to DRA to make it better. Recent research into "tunneling"—the act of throwing consecutive pitches that appear similar from a batter's point of view until after the swing decision point–data has given us a new contextual factor to account for in DRA: plate distance. This refers to the distance between successive pitches as they approach the plate, and while it has a smaller effect than factors like velocity or whiff rate, it still can help explain pitcher strikeout rate in our model.

New Pitching Metrics for 2020

We're including a few "new" pitching metrics in the book for the 2020 edition, though unlike last year, these numbers may be a little bit more familiar to those of you who have spent some time investigating baseball statistics.

Fastball Percentage

Our fastball percentage (FB%) statistic measures how frequently a pitcher throws a pitch classified as a "fastball," measured as a percentage of overall pitches thrown. We qualify three types of fastballs:

1. The traditional four-seam fastball;
2. The two-seam fastball or sinker;
3. "Hard cutters," which are pitches that have the movement profile of a cut fastball and are used as the pitcher's primary offering or in place of a more traditional fastball.

For example, a pitcher with a FB% of 67 throws any combination of these three pitches about two-thirds of the time.

Whiff Rate

Everybody loves a swing and a miss, and whiff rate (WHF) measures how frequently pitchers induce a swinging strike. To calculate WHF, we add up all the pitches thrown that ended with a swinging strike, then divide that number by a pitcher's total pitches thrown. Most often, high whiff rates correlate with high strikeout rates (and overall effective pitcher performance).

Called Strike Probability

Called Strike Probability (CSP) is a number that represents the likelihood that all of a pitcher's pitches will be called a strike while controlling for location, pitcher and batter handedness, umpire and count. Here's how it works: on each pitch, our model determines how many times (out of 100) that a similar pitch was called for a strike given those factors mentioned above, and when normalized for each batter's strike zone. Then we average the CSP for all pitches thrown by a pitcher in a season, and that gives us the yearly CSP percentage you see in the stats boxes.

As you might imagine, pitchers with a higher CSP are more likely to work in the zone, where pitchers with a lower CSP are likely locating their pitches outside the normal strike zone, for better or for worse.

Projections

Many of you aren't turning to this book just for a look at what a player has done, but for a look at what a player is going to do: the PECOTA projections. PECOTA, initially developed by Nate Silver (who has moved on to greater fame as a political analyst), consists of three parts:

1. Major-league equivalencies, which use minor-league statistics to project how a player will perform in the major leagues;
2. Baseline forecasts, which use weighted averages and regression to the mean to estimate a player's current true talent level; and
3. Aging curves, which uses the career paths of comparable players to estimate how a player's statistics are likely to change over time.

With all those important things covered, let's take a look at what's in the book this year.

Team Prospectus

Most of this book is composed of team chapters, with one for each of the 30 major-league franchises. On the first page of each chapter, you'll see a box that contains some of the key statistics for each team as well as a very inviting stadium diagram. (You can see an example of this for the Milwaukee Brewers on this very page!)

We start with the team name, their unadjusted 2019 win-loss record, and their divisional ranking. Beneath that are a host of other team statistics. **Pythag** presents an adjusted 2019 winning percentage, calculated by taking runs scored per game (**RS/G**) and runs allowed per game (**RA/G**) for the team, and running them through a version of Bill James' Pythagorean formula that was refined and improved by David Smyth and Brandon Heipp. (The formula is called "Pythagenpat," which is equally fun to type and to say.)

Next up is **DRC+**, described earlier, to indicate the overall hitting ability of the team either above or below league-average. Run prevention on the pitching side is covered by **DRA** (also mentioned earlier) and another metric: Fielding Independent Pitching (**FIP**), which calculates another ERA-like statistic based on strikeouts, walks, and home runs recorded. Defensive Efficiency Rating (**DER**) tells us the percentage of balls in play turned into outs for the team, and is a quick fielding shorthand that rounds out run prevention.

After that, we have several measures related to roster composition, as opposed to on-field performance. **B-Age** and **P-Age** tell us the average age of a team's batters and pitchers, respectively. **Salary** is the combined team payroll for all on-field players, and Doug Pappas' Marginal Dollars per Marginal Win (**M$/MW**) tells us how much money a team spent to earn production above replacement level.

Ending this batch of statistics is the number of disabled list days a team had over the season (**IL Days**) and the amount of salary paid to players on the disabled list (**$ on IL**); this final number is expressed as a percentage of total payroll.

Next to each of these stats, we've listed each team's MLB rank in that category from first to 30th. In this, first always indicates a positive outcome and 30th a negative outcome, except in the case of salary—first is highest.

After the franchise statistics, we share a few items about the team's home ballpark. There's the aforementioned diagram of the park's dimensions (including distances to the outfield wall), a graphic showing the height of the wall from the left-field pole to the right-field pole, and a table showing three-year park factors for the stadium. The park factors are displayed as indexes where 100 is average, 110 means that the park inflates the statistic in question by 10 percent, and 90 means that the park deflates the statistic in question by 10 percent.

On the second page of each team chapter, you'll find three graphs. The first is the **2019 Hit List Ranking**. This shows our Hit List Rank for the team on each day of the 2019 season and is intended to give you a picture of the ups and downs of the team's season. Hit List Rank measures overall team performance and drives the Hit List Power Rankings at the baseballprospectus.com website.

The second graph is **Committed Payroll** and helps you see how the team's payroll has compared to the MLB and divisional average payrolls over time. Payroll figures are current as of January 1, 2020; with so many free agents still unsigned as of this writing, the final 2020 figure will likely be significantly different for many teams. (In the meantime, you can always find the most current data at Baseball Prospectus' Cot's Baseball Contracts page.)

The third graph is **Farm System Ranking** and displays how the Baseball Prospectus prospect team has ranked the organization's farm system since 2007.

After the graphs, we have a **Personnel** section that lists many of the important decision-makers and upper-level field and operations staff members for the franchise, as well as any former Baseball Prospectus staff members who are currently part of the organization. (In very rare circumstances, someone might be on both lists!)

www.baseballprospectus.com

Juan Soto LF

Born: 10/25/98 Age: 21 Bats: L Throws: L
Height: 6'1" Weight: 185 Origin: International Free Agent, 2015

YEAR	TEAM	LVL	AGE	PA	R	2B	3B	HR	RBI	BB	K	SB	CS	AVG/OBP/SLG
2017	NAT	RK	18	27	3	1	1	0	4	2	1	0	0	.320/.370/.440
2017	HAG	A	18	96	15	5	0	3	14	10	8	1	2	.360/.427/.523
2018	HAG	A	19	74	12	5	3	5	24	14	13	2	0	.373/.486/.814
2018	POT	A+	19	73	17	3	1	7	18	11	8	0	1	.371/.466/.790
2018	HAR	AA	19	35	4	2	0	2	10	4	7	1	0	.323/.400/.581
2018	WAS	MLB	19	494	77	25	1	22	70	79	99	5	2	.292/.406/.517
2019	WAS	MLB	20	659	110	32	5	34	110	108	132	12	1	.282/.401/.548
2020	WAS	MLB	21	630	92	30	3	35	102	85	123	5	2	.284/.382/.543

Comparables: Ronald Acuña Jr., Mike Trout, Tony Conigliaro

YEAR	TEAM	LVL	AGE	PA	DRC+	VORP	BABIP	BRR	FRAA	WARP
2017	NAT	RK	18	27	135	1.5	.333	0.0	RF(9): -1.1	0.0
2017	HAG	A	18	96	181	8.0	.373	1.0	RF(19): -1.9, LF(2): -0.3	0.9
2018	HAG	A	19	74	222	14.5	.405	0.3	RF(14): 1.1, CF(2): 0.2	1.2
2018	POT	A+	19	73	260	15.4	.340	1.4	RF(14): 1.0, LF(1): 0.0	1.6
2018	HAR	AA	19	35	113	3.6	.364	0.0	LF(4): 0.6, RF(4): -0.5	0.1
2018	WAS	MLB	19	494	125	40.5	.338	-0.5	LF(114): 2.7	3.0
2019	WAS	MLB	20	659	136	49.0	.312	1.4	LF(150): -0.8	4.9
2020	WAS	MLB	21	630	133	43.6	.310	-0.1	LF 3	4.8

Position Players

After all that information and a thoughtful bylined essay covering each team, we present our player comments. These are also bylined, but due to frequent franchise shifts during the offseason, our bylines are more a rough guide than a perfect accounting of who wrote what.

Each player is listed with the major-league team that employed him as of early January 2020. If a player changed teams after that point via free agency, trade, or any other method, you'll be able to find them in the chapter for their previous squad.

As an example, take a look at the player comment for Nationals outfielder Juan Soto: the stat block that accompanies his written comment is at the top of this page. First we cover biographical information (age is as of June 30, 2020) before moving onto the stats themselves. Our statistic columns include standard identifying information like **YEAR**, **TEAM**, **LVL** (level of affiliated play) and **AGE** before getting into the numbers. Next, we provide raw, untranslated numbers like you might find on the back of your dad's baseball cards: **PA** (plate appearances), **R** (runs), **2B** (doubles), **3B** (triples), **HR** (home runs), **RBI** (runs batted in), **BB** (walks), **K** (strikeouts), **SB** (stolen bases) and **CS** (caught stealing).

Statistical Introduction - xi

Next, we have unadjusted "slash" statistics: **AVG** (batting average), **OBP** (on-base percentage) and **SLG** (slugging percentage). Following the slash line is **DRC+** (Deserved Runs Created Plus), which we described earlier as total offensive expected contribution compared to the league average.

One of our oldest active metrics, **VORP** (Value Over Replacement Player), considers offensive production, position and plate appearances. In essence, it is the number of runs contributed beyond what a replacement-level player at the same position would contribute if given the same percentage of team plate appearances. VORP does not consider the quality of a player's defense.

BABIP (batting average on balls in play) tells us how often a ball in play fell for a hit, and can help us identify whether a batter may have been lucky or not...but note that high BABIPs also tend to follow the great hitters of our time, as well as speedy singles hitters who put the ball on the ground.

The next item is **BRR** (Baserunning Runs), which covers all of a player's baserunning accomplishments including (but not limited to) swiped bags and failed attempts. Next is **FRAA** (Fielding Runs Above Average), which also includes the number of games previously played at each position noted in parentheses. Multi-position players have only their two most frequent positions listed here, but their total FRAA number reflects all positions played.

Our last column here is **WARP** (Wins Above Replacement Player). WARP estimates the total value of a player, which means for hitters it takes into account hitting runs above average (calculated using the DRC+ model), BRR and FRAA. Then, it makes an adjustment for positions played and gives the player a credit for plate appearances based upon the difference between "replacement level"—which is derived from the quality of players added to a team's roster after the start of the season–and the league average.

The final line just below the stats box is **PECOTA** data, which is discussed further in a following section.

Catchers

Catchers are a special breed, and thus they have earned their own separate box which displays some of the defensive metrics that we've built just for them. As an example, let's check out J.T. Realmuto.

The **YEAR** and **TEAM** columns match what you'd find in the other stat box. **P. COUNT** indicates the number of pitches thrown while the catcher was behind the plate, including swinging strikes, fouls and balls in play. **FRM RUNS** is the total run value the catcher provided (or cost) his team by influencing the umpire to call strikes where other catchers did not. **BLK RUNS** expresses the total run value above or below average for the catcher's ability to prevent wild pitches and passed balls. **THRW RUNS** is calculated using a similar model as the previous two statistics, and it measures a catcher's ability to throw out basestealers but also to dissuade them from testing his arm in the first place. It takes into account factors like the pitcher (including his delivery and pickoff move) and baserunner (who could be as fast as Billy Hamilton or as slow as Yonder Alonso). **TOT RUNS** is the sum of all of the previous three statistics.

Justin Verlander RHP
Born: 02/20/83 Age: 37 Bats: R Throws: R
Height: 6'5" Weight: 225 Origin: Round 1, 2004 Draft (#2 overall)

YEAR	TEAM	LVL	AGE	W	L	SV	G	GS	IP	H	HR	BB/9	K/9	K	GB%	BABIP
2017	DET	MLB	34	10	8	0	28	28	172	153	23	3.5	9.2	176	34%	.283
2017	HOU	MLB	34	5	0	0	5	5	34	17	4	1.3	11.4	43	32%	.194
2018	HOU	MLB	35	16	9	0	34	34	214	156	28	1.6	12.2	290	31%	.272
2019	HOU	MLB	36	21	6	0	34	34	223	137	36	1.7	12.1	300	36%	.219
2020	HOU	MLB	37	15	6	0	29	29	184	138	28	2.3	12.1	248	35%	.274

Comparables: Zack Greinke, A.J. Burnett, Aníbal Sánchez

YEAR	TEAM	LVL	AGE	WHIP	ERA	DRA	WARP	MPH	FB%	WHF	CSP
2017	DET	MLB	34	1.28	3.82	4.03	3.0	97.7	58	11	47.8
2017	HOU	MLB	34	0.65	1.06	3.08	0.9	97.5	59.6	15.1	49.9
2018	HOU	MLB	35	0.90	2.52	2.33	7.3	97.5	61.2	16.2	51.6
2019	HOU	MLB	36	0.80	2.58	2.51	7.9	96.8	49.9	17.5	48.3
2020	HOU	MLB	37	1.01	2.75	2.95	5.3	95.8	54.6	15.1	48.2

Pitchers

Let's give our pitchers a turn, using 2019 AL Cy Young winner Justin Verlander as our example. Take a look at his stat block: the first line and the **YEAR**, **TEAM**, **LVL** and **AGE** columns are the same as in the position player example earlier.

Here too, we have a series of columns that display raw, unadjusted statistics compiled by the pitcher over the course of a season: **W** (wins), **L** (losses), **SV** (saves), **G** (games pitched), **GS** (games started), **IP** (innings pitched), **H** (hits allowed) and **HR** (home runs allowed). Next we have two statistics that are rates: **BB/9** (walks per nine innings) and **K/9** (strikeouts per nine innings), before returning to the unadjusted K (strikeouts).

Next up is **GB%** (ground ball percentage), which is the percentage of all batted balls that were hit on the ground, including both outs and hits. Remember, this is based on observational data and subject to human error, so please approach this with a healthy dose of skepticism.

BABIP (batting average on balls in play) is calculated using the same methodology as it is for position players, but it often tells us more about a pitcher than it does a hitter. With pitchers, a high BABIP is often due to poor defense or bad luck, and can often be an indicator of potential rebound, and a low BABIP may be cause to expect performance regression. (A typical league-average BABIP is close to .290-.300.)

Boston Red Sox 2020

The metrics **WHIP** (walks plus hits per inning pitched) and **ERA** (earned run average) are old standbys: WHIP measures walks and hits allowed on a per-inning basis, while ERA measures earned runs on a nine-inning basis. Neither of these stats are translated or adjusted.

DRA (Deserved Run Average) was described at length earlier, and measures how many runs the pitcher "deserved" to allow per nine innings. Please note that since we lack all the data points that would make for a "real" DRA for minor-league events, the DRA displayed for minor league partial-seasons is based off of different data. (That data is a modified version of our cFIP metric, which you can find more information about on our website.)

Just like with hitters, **WARP** (Wins Above Replacement Player) is a total value metric that puts pitchers of all stripes on the same scale as position players. We use DRA as the primary input for our calculation of WARP. You might notice that relief pitchers (due to their limited innings) may have a lower WARP than you were expecting or than you might see in other WARP-like metrics. WARP does not take leverage into account, just the actions a pitcher performs and the expected value of those actions...which ends up judging high-leverage relief pitchers differently than you might imagine given their prestige and market value.

MPH gives you the pitcher's 95th percentile velocity for the noted season, in order to give you an idea of what the *peak* fastball velocity a pitcher possesses. Since this comes from our pitch-tracking data, it is not publicly available for minor-league pitchers.

Finally, we display the three new pitching metrics we described earlier. **FB%** (fastball percentage) gives you the percentage of fastballs thrown out of all pitches. **WHF** (whiff rate) tells you the percentage of swinging strikes induced out of all pitches. **CSP** (called strike probability) expresses the likelihood of all pitches thrown to result in a called strike, after controlling for factors like handedness, umpire, pitch type, count and location.

PECOTA

All players have PECOTA projections for 2020, as well as a set of other numbers that describe the performance of comparable players according to PECOTA. All projections for 2020 are for the player at the date we went to press in early January and are projected into the league and park context as indicated by the team abbreviation. (Note that players at very low levels of the minors are too unpredictable to assess using these numbers.) All PECOTA projected statistics represent a player's projected major-league performance.

Below the projections are the player's three highest-scoring comparable players as determined by PECOTA. All comparables represent a snapshot of how the listed player was performing at the same age as the current player, so if a

23-year-old pitcher is compared to Bartolo Colón, he's actually being compared to a 23-year-old Colón, not the version that pitched for the Rangers in 2018, nor to Colón's career as a whole.

A few points about pitcher projections. First, we aren't yet projecting peak velocity, so that column will be blank in the PECOTA lines. Second, projecting DRA is trickier than evaluating past performance, because it is unclear how deserving each pitcher will be of his anticipated outcomes. However, we know that another DRA-related statistic–contextual FIP or cFIP-estimates future run scoring very well. So for PECOTA, the projected DRA figures you see are based on the past cFIPs generated by the pitcher and comparable players over time, along with the other factors described above.

Lineouts

In each chapter's Lineouts section, you'll find abbreviated text comments, as well as all the same information you'd find in our full player comments. The only difference is that we limit the stats boxes in this section to only including the 2019 information for each player.

Managers

After all those wonderful team chapters, we've got statistics for each big-league manager, all of whom are organized by alphabetical order. Here you'll find a block including an extraordinary amount of information collected from each manager's entire career. For more information on the acronyms and what they mean, please visit the Glossary at www.baseballprospectus.com.

There is one important metric that we'd like to call attention to, and you'll find it next to each manager's name: **wRM+** (weighted reliever management plus). Developed by Rob Arthur and Rian Watt, wRM+ investigates how good a manager is at using their best relievers during the moments of highest leverage, using both our proprietary DRA metric as well as Leverage Index. wRM+ is scaled to a league average of 100, and a wRM+ of 105 indicates that relievers were used approximately five percent "better" than average. On the other hand, a wRM+ of 95 would tell us the team used its relievers five percent "worse" than the average team.

While wRM+ does not have an extremely strong correlation with a manager, it is statistically significant; this means that a manager is not *entirely* responsible for a team's wRM+, but does have some effect on that number.

PECOTA Leaderboards

If you're familiar with PECOTA, then you'll have noticed that the projection system often appears bullish on players coming off a bad year and bearish on players coming off a good year. (This is because the system weights several previous seasons, not just the most recent one.) In addition, we publish the 50th

Boston Red Sox 2020

percentile projections for each player—which is smack in the middle of the range of projected production—which tends to mean PECOTA stat lines don't often have extreme results like 40 home runs or 250 strikeouts in a given season. In essence, PECOTA doesn't project very many extreme seasons.

At the end of the book, we've ranked the top players at each position based on their PECOTA projections. This might help you visualize just how a given player's projection compares to that of their peers, so that even if a dramatic stat line isn't projected, you can still imagine how they stack up against the rest of the league.

Part 1: Team Analysis

Boston Red Sox: Where Are You Going, Where Have You Been?

Scott Orgera, Alexis Collins and Matthew Trueblood

2019: What Went Right

Prior to the 2019 season, PECOTA projected the Red Sox to go 90-72. It seemed to be a conservative forecast given that they notched 108 wins in 2018. In reality, the Red Sox underplayed even that pessimistic assessment and finished 84-78. The reasons for this precipitous nosedive were many, some of which the front office probably should have seen coming. Still, there were redeeming factors, mainly a lineup that was downright explosive at times and kept things interesting during a few brief stretches.

The Boston offense accounted for 29.4 WARP, good for fifth in the majors behind four playoff-bound clubs in the Astros, Dodgers, Twins and Braves. The Boston bats also ranked among baseball's leaders in DRC+ (4th: 108), OPS (5th: .806) and AVG (3rd: .269), thanks to a balanced attack that did more than just crush homers. A trio of All-Stars joined forces with a baby-faced third baseman to account for the lion's share of the team's run production. Veteran slugger J.D. Martinez picked up right where he had left off in '18. Mookie Betts was a top-tier player yet again, good enough for a team-high 6.9 WARP. Xander Bogaerts, already in his seventh season at 26, had his best campaign yet. Though defensive metrics disagree greatly on the value he's providing, Bogaerts' real value comes at the dish where he contributed a 134 DRC+. Rafael Devers raised his OPS almost 200 points from the previous season and led the league in doubles (54) and total bases (359). Boston's backstop also deserves some love: Once thought of as only a part-time player, Christian Vázquez played well over 100 games behind the plate and compiled 106 DRC+ and 4.2 WARP with a career-high 23 bombs.

As a group, the starting pitchers were an unmitigated disaster but there was a bright spot amidst the ranks. It wasn't one of the high-paid marquee names atop the rotation. While everything else was falling apart around him, Eduardo

Rodríguez had a banner season, going 19-6 with a 3.81 ERA in a league-leading 34 starts with 213 strikeouts in 203 1/3 innings. The left-hander's WARP (2.9) ranked second behind ace Chris Sale (4.5).

Not much can be said about the bullpen under this heading except that it was a 31-year-old who doesn't throw particularly hard and relies heavily on a curveball who was most effective when it mattered: Brandon Workman's 1.88 ERA was almost two runs better than any other on the staff. He also led the team in FIP (2.46), had the best WARP of their relief corps and struck out 13 batters per nine innings.

2019: **What Went Wrong**

Boston's roster was largely identical to the one that dispatched the mighty Dodgers in five World Series games. Attempting to mitigate the shortened winter break, manager Alex Cora made sure four-fifths of the starting rotation hardly pitched at all in spring training. It wasn't necessarily fatigue that the club had to fear, but roster decisions made during the offseason. The main concern surrounding Cora's club entering the season was its bullpen depth, or lack thereof. Craig Kimbrel was gone, left to over-ripen on the free agent market, while Joe Kelly: Postseason Hero departed for the team he abused in the World Series, and a plum $25 million contract. Letting them go was defensible. Less so was the decision, despite their many resources, not to replace them. This left a substantial void in the late innings. The plan was to use a hodgepodge of internal options such as Workman, Ryan Brasier, and Matt Barnes, to fill those vacated spots, but even if they could, this neglected the knock-on effect of moving the trio to higher-leverage innings: Who was supposed to cover the key innings they had taken in 2018?

Erstwhile President of Baseball Operations Dave Dombrowski brought in mediocre free agents that included three-time PED offender Jenrry Mejia to compete with a cast of other journeymen like Erasmo Ramírez and Carson Smith, hoping that one or more would pan out. What looked like a simple proposal at first glance was actually a convoluted one, and to no one's surprise relying on a bunch of "what if's" backfired, forcing Cora to spend the summer mixing and matching with mostly ineffective options.

Boston's relief woes were minor compared to the struggles of the starting five. Sale was probably the biggest disappointment, going 6-11 with a career-high 4.40 ERA in 25 starts. His FIP and DRA were 3.41 and 3.00, respectively, so the lopsided record wasn't all his doing but reflected a lack of defensive support. The 30-year-old also posted a 13.3 K/9 ratio, right around his Red Sox average. Nevertheless, Sale's health limited him to the lowest number of innings (147 1/3) he's ever thrown as a starter and the results spoke for themselves. Sale was shut down for the season in mid-August due to lingering left elbow issues, receiving a PRP injection from Dr. James Andrews shortly after.

Fellow southpaw David Price didn't fare much better and was also shut down early with wrist problems. The former Cy Young Award winner and 2018's AL Comeback Player of the Year had a terrific first half, going 7-2 with a 3.24 ERA, fanning 95 in 83 1/3 innings. Not unlike the team itself, Price fell flat on his face coming out of the All-Star break, posting a 7.88 ERA in 24 frames—a stretch of six starts over which he walked 11 and surrendered eight homers. Another ex-Cy Young champ, Rick Porcello was awful despite a winning record. The Red Sox paid $21 million for the pleasure of his company, then watched him decamp for the Mets.

Perhaps Dombrowski's biggest blunder was re-signing Nathan Eovaldi to a four-year, $68 million contract following a heroic October. Predictably, the postseason magic didn't carry over, with the always-friable Eovaldi missing three-plus months after April elbow surgery. Ten-year vet Andrew Cashner joined the fray in a July swap with Baltimore but added little.

Things were tough out of the gate for Boston, having to dig out of a 6-13 hole and slipping on a banana peel each time it looked like they were about to turn a corner and pull themselves within striking distance of a wild-card spot. Then there was the stretch of eight losses in a row to the division-rival Rays and Yankees in late July and early August, a week that started with the Sox 12 games over .500 and seemingly ready to make a run. They also couldn't recapture the late-inning magic of 2018, when over 40 of their 108 regular season victories were of the come-from-behind variety, a theme that continued in the postseason.

All of this led to the firing of Dombrowski only a season removed from a championship, and his subsequent replacement by Chaim Bloom of the Rays. At this writing, the team is also without a manager due to Cora's involvement in the Astros' sign-stealing scandal. —*Scott Orgera*

Prospect Outlook

There wasn't much of promise on the Boston farm until after the draft. When the Red Sox brought in Dombrowski they knew he would prioritize constructing the most competitive major league roster at the expense of the farm system. As a result, his replacement has some work to do. There were, however, some strong individual performances: Top prospect **Michael Chavis** spent most of spring training with the major-league team before he was sent down to start the season at Triple-A. He played only 21 games before he was needed in the majors. He filled in at both first and second while also contributing offensively, at least early on.

Tristan Casas, the team's 2018 first-round pick, played 120 games in the Carolina League, after only playing two games the year before due to injury. The erstwhile third baseman spent the majority of the season at first. He's still a few years away from the majors, but his first full season suggested that he could still provide value despite the defensive downgrade. Scouts are still enamored with his bat, even with the .254 average at Low-A. **Bobby Dalbec** spent most of the season in Double-A Portland, before earning a call-up to Triple-A for the last month of the season. While Dalbec is likely to start 2020 back in Triple-A, the Red Sox will have to find space for him with Devers at third base and Chavis having a prior claim on playing time at first and second. While his Three True Outcomes approach worked in Double-A, his brief stint in Triple-A didn't go quite so smoothly even with the jumpier ball.

The most notable story out of the 2019 draft was fourth-round pick RHP **Noah Song**, drafted out of the Naval Academy. He impressed scouts this season, but his future is uncertain given a commitment to service that the Navy has declined to defer. RHP **Tanner Houck** got a spring training NRI and his fastball-slider combination will probably grace the bullpen at some point this season. RHP **Thad Ward** will start the season in Portland where he'll attempt to show that his future is in the rotation rather than the bullpen. His deep arsenal would seem to argue for the former. RHP **Bryan Mata** is in a similar position, possessing a mid-90s fastball but a concerning lack of command. Change is coming to the Red Sox organization and one of the highest priorities for the new regime will be to rebuild the farm system. Whether through trades or the draft, the team will need to develop some arms to be able to compete for another championship. —*Alexis Collins*

2020 Outlook

As disappointing as their 2019 season was, the Sox undeniably had a championship core on hand, and that makes the way they conducted themselves this winter a double disgrace. New GM Chaim Bloom was hired because he is an experienced and willing executor of the wills and whims of ownership. In Boston's case, this winter, that meant offloading enough salary to solve the non-problem that cropped up in the wake of the team winning the 2018 World Series: their hefty payroll.

Bloom started without much leverage and did a poor job of maintaining it. To a team that badly needed real help at the margins, he gave only warm bodies for reinforcement: Martín Pérez for the back end of the rotation, José Peraza for the bench role previously filled by the better but more expensive Holt, and Mitch Moreland (again) for the vacant half of a cold-corner platoon. The writing was on the wall. The Sox sat out the portion of the winter during which they could have gotten better, as they went about the important business of getting cheaper and worse.

For Betts and Price (plus over $40 million in salary relief), Bloom netted Alex Verdugo, Jeter Downs and Connor Wong. Verdugo projects to take over as an everyday outfielder, and he's not a bad one—but calling him a good one might be a bit of a reach. Verdugo fills Betts's place only slightly better than John Wasdin filled that of Roger Clemens. Downs and Wong represent an improved prospect haul over the earlier iteration of the trade that involved the Twins and Brusdar Graterol.

There's no reason the Red Sox can't compete in 2020. They still have a tremendously talented roster. However, they've struck a blow to their own fanbase, and they've moved on voluntarily from a franchise icon, and Bloom only did as well as his circumstances allowed. —*Matthew Trueblood*

Performance Graphs

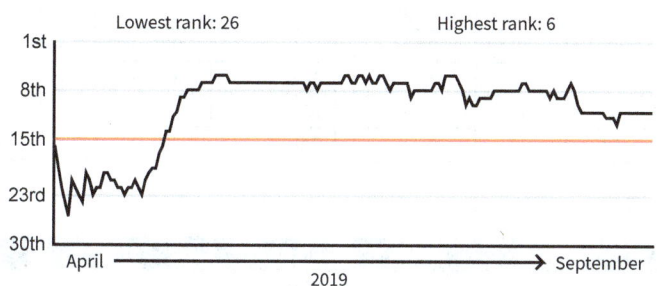

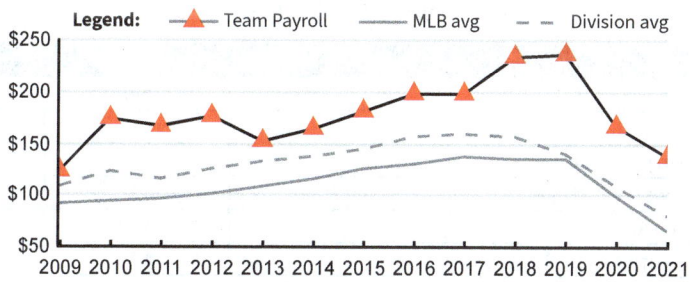

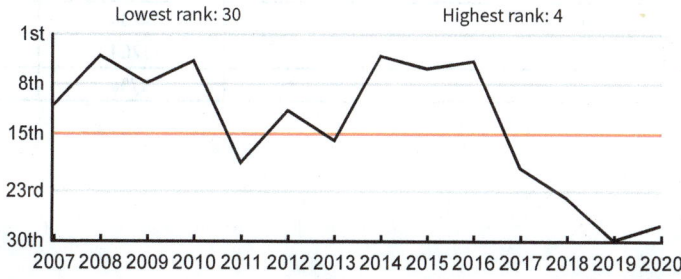

2019 Team Performance

ACTUAL STANDINGS

Team	W	L	Pct
NYA	103	59	0.636
TBA	96	66	0.593
BOS	**84**	**78**	**0.519**
TOR	67	95	0.414
BAL	54	108	0.333

THIRD-ORDER STANDINGS

Team	W	L	Pct
TBA	99	63	0.613
NYA	96	66	0.590
BOS	**88**	**74**	**0.544**
TOR	66	96	0.410
BAL	59	103	0.363

TOP HITTERS

Player	WARP
Mookie Betts	6.9
Rafael Devers	5.6
Xander Bogaerts	4.3

TOP PITCHERS

Player	WARP
Chris Sale	4.5
Eduardo Rodriguez	2.9
Brandon Workman	1.9

VITAL STATISTICS

Statistic Name	Value	Rank
Pythagenpat	.542	12th
Runs Scored per Game	5.56	4th
Runs Allowed per Game	5.11	20th
Deserved Runs Created Plus	108	4th
Deserved Run Average	4.92	16th
Fielding Independent Pitching	4.31	12th
Defensive Efficiency Rating	.688	27th
Batter Age	27.2	4th
Pitcher Age	28.9	23rd
Salary	$236.2M	1st
Marginal $ per Marginal Win	$6.3M	6th
Injured List Days	1204	19th
$ on IL	17%	19th

2020 Team Projections

PROJECTED STANDINGS

Team	W	L	Pct	+/-
NYA	99.0	63.0	0.611	-4
TBA	87.3	74.7	0.539	-9
BOS	**84.5**	**77.5**	**0.522**	**0**
TOR	76.6	85.4	0.473	10
BAL	62.9	99.1	0.388	9

TOP PROJECTED HITTERS

Player	WARP
J.D. Martinez	4.3
Rafael Devers	3.6
Xander Bogaerts	3.5

TOP PROJECTED PITCHERS

Player	WARP
Chris Sale	4.7
Eduardo Rodriguez	1.2
Nathan Eovaldi	1.0

FARM SYSTEM REPORT

Top Prospect	Number of Top 101 Prospects
Triston Casas	0

KEY DEDUCTIONS

Player	WARP
Mookie Betts	6.6
David Price	2.2
Rick Porcello	0.7
Jhoulys Chacín	0.2
Sandy León	0.0
Sam Travis	-0.1
Travis Lakins	-0.2
Trevor Kelley	-0.2

KEY ADDITIONS

Player	WARP
Alex Verdugo	1.9
Kevin Plawecki	0.6
José Peraza	0.4
Bobby Dalbec	0.2
Marcus Wilson	0.1
Martín Pérez	0.1
Yoan Aybar	0.1
Kyle Hart	0.1
Kevin Pillar	0.0
C.J. Chatham	0.0

Team Personnel

Chief Baseball Officer
Chaim Bloom

Executive Vice President/Assistant General Manager
Zack Scott

Executive Vice President/Assistant General Manager
Raquel Ferreira

Vice President, Player Development
Ben Crockett

Manager
Ron Roenicke

BP Alumni
Chaim Bloom
Todd Gold
Tyler Oringer

Fenway Park Stats

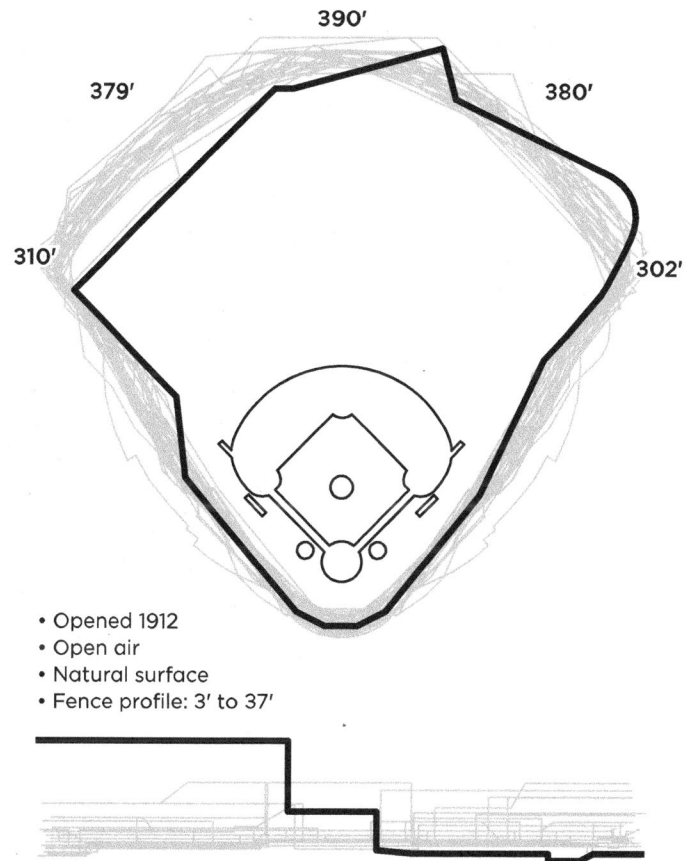

- Opened 1912
- Open air
- Natural surface
- Fence profile: 3' to 37'

Three-Year Park Factors

Runs	Runs/RH	Runs/LH	HR/RH	HR/LH
103	104	102	97	91

Red Sox Team Analysis

Just over 18 years ago, the Red Sox changed ownership. For nearly seven decades, the franchise had been in the hands (and then the family) of Tom Yawkey, who had bought the club in 1933 for $1.25 million—about $24 million in today's money—and ran it until his death in 1977. Under Yawkey, the Red Sox were sporadically good, mixing long stretches of mediocrity and outright awfulness with transcendent bursts of contention that inevitably ended in excruciating World Series losses. (Yawkey also threw in some racism that was egregious even by the standards of the time: Boston was the last team to integrate, doing so in 1959, and only grudgingly, having famously passed on a chance to sign Jackie Robinson in 1945.)

After Yawkey's death, his wife Jean took over until she passed away in 1992, at which point the team was run by a trust set up in the family name. They carried on Yawkey's legacy of blending intermittent highs with a smooth paste of third-place finishes and 81-win seasons. But no matter the Hall-of-Fame talents who passed through Fenway Park—Ted Williams, Carl Yastrzemski, Carlton Fisk, Pedro Martínez, the four weeks of the season during which Brian Daubach hit like peak Barry Bonds—the end result was always the same: no championship.

By the end of the 2001 season, the Red Sox hadn't won a pennant in 15 years or a World Series in nearly a century. A miasma of bad feelings created by petty, internecine squabbles and ill-considered moves (or non-moves, occasionally) hung over the team, broken up only by Martínez's starts. At the same time, there were persistent rumors that the club was going to tear down Fenway—the lyrical little bandbox of John Updike's prose that nonetheless fit only 35,000 people and was about as comfortable to sit in as a porta-potty—and leave Boston proper. The present was uninspiring; the future was bleak.

Then along came John W. Henry. Tall, thin and nearly translucent, Henry made his millions as a commodities trader but always harbored a dream of owning a baseball team. He managed to gain sole control of the then-Florida Marlins in the late 1990s, but that was the equivalent of buying a gutted house. A better opportunity presented itself in 2001, when the Red Sox went on the block.

Joining former Padres CEO Larry Lucchino and television producer Tom Werner, Henry became the money man for a group who, before he jumped on board, was a relative long shot to purchase the team. (The favorite at the time was Frank McCourt, who went on to buy and almost destroy the Dodgers; I think about the alternate universe where he takes over the Red Sox at least four times a week.) With Henry footing the majority of the bill, the new group took over on Dec. 20, 2001, for a price tag of $695 million, and committed to staying in the city and Fenway.

Within three years of taking over, Henry and company built the Red Sox into something most fans in New England figured the team would never be: a world champion. A second title followed in 2007, then another in '13, and a fourth in '18. Almost overnight, baseball's perpetual bridesmaid became this millennium's version of the Yankees, in the process (and along with the Patriots) turning Boston from America's most insufferable sports city into America's most insufferable and successful sports city.

All the while, as the team took its place among MLB's elite, Henry kept footing the bill, spending millions upon millions of dollars to ensure a winning club and also to establish the Red Sox as a money-making machine. The two went hand-in-hand: No one will repeatedly spend their hard-earned paychecks to watch a loser, so Henry had to spend his to make sure that never came to pass. Beyond that, though, he understood that the club needed as many revenue streams as possible, and ideally for said streams to be diverse. So, he poured money not just into the roster but also into Fenway, the team's cable network NESN, the *Boston Globe* (which he purchased in 2013) and a sports consortium who bought Liverpool F.C. in the English Premier League and half of Roush Racing, a NASCAR team. As Henry told ESPN in 2011: "You can't win in any sport without concentrating on revenue generation. You have to be relentless in that regard if you are going to be able to afford the kind of players you need to compete at the highest level. There is simply no way around that."

Which brings us to 2019, and the apparent end of the John Henry gravy train. The architect of Boston's last championship club was Dave Dombrowski, a man renowned in baseball for his ability to spend other people's money to build a winner. He did that in Florida; came within a whisker of doing so several times in Detroit; and, just three years after being appointed the president of baseball operations for the Red Sox, pulled off the feat once more. The 2018 team was one of the best in franchise history, steamrolling all comers en route to 108 wins, a pennant and a World Series. Yet all that bought Dombrowski was another 11 months: With the 2019 team struggling to repeat the previous year's dominance, he was fired in September.

Six weeks later, the Red Sox hired his replacement: Chaim Bloom, late of the Rays. With Tampa Bay, Bloom had established himself as a forward thinker, helping the team develop a reputation as a Silicon Valley-style disruptor. What was likely more important to Henry and company, though, was Bloom's environment—which is to say, that Tampa Bay won despite running payrolls that barely cracked $60 million. For a club who had spent $240 million in exchange for 84 wins and a third-place finish behind Bloom's Rays, the idea of winning without spending probably held plenty of appeal.

So it is that the 2020 Red Sox, with Bloom at the forefront, will join the rest of baseball in worshipping at the altar of Sustainability and Financial Flexibility, and all the other buzzwords dragged in from the finance world that now acts as a pipeline to front offices. In theory and in the press conferences, that's presented as a kind of ideal contention state in which a team is composed entirely of 26-year-old players putting up 8-WARP seasons for no more than $2 million per person. It's a farm system that never stops producing; prospects who never fail; free-agent and trade decisions that never go wrong because they're made with minimal emotion and maximum attention to the cold, hard reality of aging curves and predictive models.

That's the dream, anyway. The reality is far simpler: less spending. The teams who preach sustainability are selling a dressed-up version of belt-tightening, in which free agency is more or less ignored and contract extensions done only if a player is willing to take 75 percent of his value. The majority of the money a team makes is no longer poured into payroll, in part because the majority of the money a team makes now is no longer tied to anything affected by payroll. Like Henry, MLB and its teams have spent the last decade or so diversifying their revenue streams, and in the process, they've largely divorced profit from the actual games being played on the field. Cable networks, streaming packages, stadium deals, corporate sponsorships: Those are what bring in the money, and those stay steady whether a team wins 100 games or 60. Ticket sales, meanwhile, continue to shrink in each club's pie chart of revenues—even as, ironically enough, ticket prices keep increasing.

The end result is a team who can now make money without spending as much of it. Like America's richest individuals and families, teams have reached a level of wealth wherein the faucet never goes dry. And like that same group firmly ensconced in the country's top 1 percent of earners, teams have committed to making sure as much of that money stays with them as is possible. Hence, the aversion to giving it to players, or at least, the aversion to giving it to players if they don't have to. That's all been helped along by the data showing the most productive years of a player's career come in his early to mid-20s; by pure coincidence, those also happen to be the cheapest years of a player's career.

The Dombrowski Red Sox weren't built with that in mind; if the linchpins of a champion happened to be earning 1/10th of what they were worth, that was a happy accident. Spending in free agency (and a willingness to trade those desirable cheap prospects for expensive stars) was the key to their success. The future of the Bloom Red Sox, though, is one wherein as much of the roster as possible is being underpaid relative to the value created. It's why rumors of a Mookie Betts trade persisted all offseason long (and will likely continue throughout the year), despite the fact that a Red Sox team without him is a Red Sox team who won't win anything at all. Betts will be a free agent after the season, and he's a lock to score $300 million-plus on the open market; a team already on the hook for nearly a quarter billion dollars in payroll this year isn't eager to add more numbers to that tally. It's also why, if Betts survives the winter still with the team who drafted him, he almost certainly won't re-sign there. Those kinds of expenditures don't fit with the concept of financial flexibility.

Sustainability promises perpetual contention. But what it amounts to is your favorite players turned into numbers, or into chess pieces to be sacrificed if necessary: Picture an Excel spreadsheet stamping on a Mookie Betts jersey, forever. Winning—a thing the Red Sox did only every now and then, and incompletely at that, before Henry became Boston's biggest sugar daddy—becomes secondary to bottom lines. This doesn't benefit the fans, who should care more about trophies than luxury tax payments. It exists for the owners—to take Henry's investment and give it a positive yield.

This is the tack many teams have taken, but for a good long while, the Red Sox resisted the siren song of spending less to win...uh, less. You don't hire Dave Dombrowski to clip coupons. And what's been admirable about Red Sox ownership under Henry, even amid the apparently universe-mandated directive that whoever's in charge of the team has to be weirdly and dismissively pissy about departing managers, GMs, players and just about everyone else, is that they've spent willingly and spent big. They shelled out $160 million for Manny Ramirez and $210 million for David Price. They acquired big-name players via trade, contract be damned. Henry easily and understandably could've snapped his checkbook shut for good after deals that went sour, like Carl Crawford and Adrián González and Hanley Ramírez and Pablo Sandoval. But he kept the dollars flowing, and for it, he's been rewarded with four championships in 18 years. The 2013 and '18 titles, in particular, don't happen unless Boston throws its financial weight around.

That's the advantage Boston is supposed to have and supposed to use. Few if any teams can match the Red Sox dollar for dollar. It's their bad luck that one of those teams so happens to reside in their division (and splurged heavily this winter for the best pitcher on the market in Gerrit Cole), but otherwise, they exist within their own layer of the atmosphere. Owning a sports team of any real sort in America is a license to print money; if you happen to be one of the lucky saps who controls a titanic, historic franchise like the Red Sox, you're basically in charge of Baseball Disneyland.

Yet that won't be the path going forward—at least, that seems like a safe bet given the hiring of Bloom and an offseason so quiet that Boston was outspent by the likes of the Blue Jays and White Sox. The track has already been laid for a pivot toward spending less. Despite the prospect of losing Betts and despite the window he helped create inching further shut, there's been no push to build the best team possible while he's still under contract. Where that ends up leaving Red Sox fans, so used to champagne and parades and lording it over Yankees fans as the most successful team of this century, remains to be seen. Maybe it works. But one thing is certain: The true beneficiary in all this is the man who, nearly two decades ago, put down more money than anyone reading this will make in 10 lifetimes to own a baseball team.

By the way, in case you were wondering, the present-day value of Fenway Sports Group—the Red Sox, Liverpool, Roush Racing, NESN, Fenway Park and much more—is $6.6 billion. Even with all the money spent on players, John Henry has more than made his money back and then some. The question going forward is what the fans are going to get out of his newfound turn toward austerity.

—Jon Tayler is a former staff writer at Sports Illustrated.

Part 2: Player Analysis

PLAYER COMMENTS WITH GRAPHS

Andrew Benintendi LF
Born: 07/06/94   Age: 25   Bats: L   Throws: L
Height: 5'10"   Weight: 170   Origin: Round 1, 2015 Draft (#7 overall)

YEAR	TEAM	LVL	AGE	PA	R	2B	3B	HR	RBI	BB	K	SB	CS	AVG/OBP/SLG
2017	BOS	MLB	22	658	84	26	1	20	90	70	112	20	5	.271/.352/.424
2018	BOS	MLB	23	661	103	41	6	16	87	71	106	21	3	.290/.366/.465
2019	BOS	MLB	24	615	72	40	5	13	68	59	140	10	3	.266/.343/.431
2020	BOS	MLB	25	595	67	39	4	17	71	58	129	13	4	.266/.343/.449

Comparables: Carl Yastrzemski, Christian Yelich, Roger Cedeno

Do we never hear about "junior slumps" because they're rarer than their sophomore counterpart, or simply because they're less alliterative? In his third full season, Benintendi set career worsts in just about every category that matters. Despite the hitter-friendly balls, his slugging percentage dropped. Despite an improved BABIP, he posted his worst batting average. He walked less and struck out more, as he chased more pitches out of the zone. He didn't run as much. And for the turd cherry on top of this poop sundae (scouting term), he even had a bad year in the field, per FRAA. If you're looking for a silver lining or two, Benny still hit the ball hard and didn't post big platoon splits. Plus, there was absolutely nothing in Benintendi's profile to suggest this type of decline in performance was around the corner, which could mean a bounce back is in store. Then again, there's no one injury, event or major change that can explain away Benintendi's poor showing either. That's got to make the Red Sox at least a little uneasy.

YEAR	TEAM	LVL	AGE	PA	DRC+	VORP	BABIP	BRR	FRAA	WARP
2017	BOS	MLB	22	658	107	18.1	.301	1.4	LF(123): -0.6, CF(30): 0.0	2.5
2018	BOS	MLB	23	661	118	33.3	.328	-1.1	LF(129): 8.2, CF(24): -2.6	3.7
2019	BOS	MLB	24	615	95	12.9	.333	0.8	LF(131): -5.7, CF(12): 1.5	0.9
2020	BOS	MLB	25	595	104	19.2	.323	-0.6	LF -3, CF -1	1.6

Andrew Benintendi, continued

Batted Ball Distribution

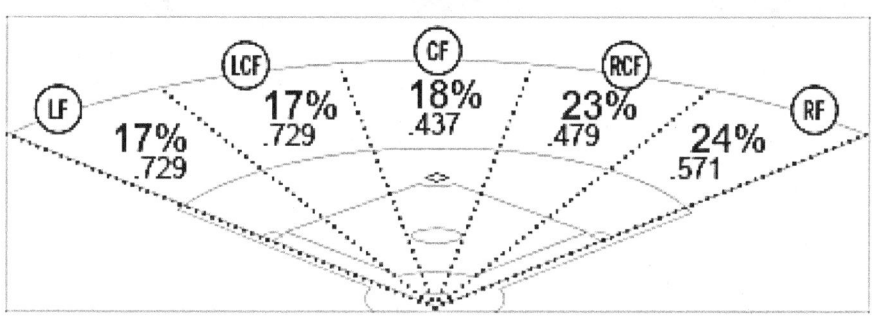

Strike Zone vs LHP   Strike Zone vs RHP

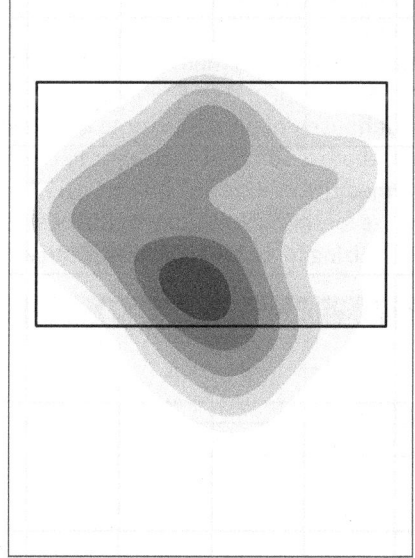

Red Sox Player Analysis - 23

Xander Bogaerts SS

Born: 10/01/92 Age: 27 Bats: R Throws: R
Height: 6'1" Weight: 210 Origin: International Free Agent, 2009

YEAR	TEAM	LVL	AGE	PA	R	2B	3B	HR	RBI	BB	K	SB	CS	AVG/OBP/SLG
2017	BOS	MLB	24	635	94	32	6	10	62	56	116	15	1	.273/.343/.403
2018	BOS	MLB	25	580	72	45	3	23	103	55	102	8	2	.288/.360/.522
2019	BOS	MLB	26	698	110	52	0	33	117	76	122	4	2	.309/.384/.555
2020	BOS	MLB	27	595	74	37	1	23	81	56	107	9	3	.285/.358/.488

Comparables: Alex Gonzalez, Derek Jeter, Starlin Castro

Only two factors prevent our metrics from indicating that Bogaerts was the best shortstop in baseball in 2019. The first is that Marcus Semien used some *Space Jam*-ass magic to post a vintage Alex Rodríguez season, and if you can explain that, well, we're all ears. The second equally mysterious but perhaps more digestible reason: Bogaerts went from an average defender to one of the league's worst overnight, per FRAA. That doesn't jive with the eye test, and if you take Bogey to a net even defender, our metrics suddenly say he's a down-ballot MVP candidate on the strength of his potent bat. The X-Man lived up to expectations and then some following his six-year contract extension, pacing the Sox in RBI and OPS while growing into more of a leadership role in the clubhouse—of particular note is his mentorship of Rafael Devers, which gives baseball its spiritual successor to the Adrían Beltré/Elvis Andrus buddy cop comedy. Now entering just his age-27 season, Bogaerts remains a foundational piece for the Sox and one of the best middle infielders in the game; a true stabilizing force for an otherwise turbulent franchise.

YEAR	TEAM	LVL	AGE	PA	DRC+	VORP	BABIP	BRR	FRAA	WARP
2017	BOS	MLB	24	635	98	31.9	.327	5.5	SS(146): -9.2	2.4
2018	BOS	MLB	25	580	130	49.6	.317	-0.2	SS(136): 1.5	4.9
2019	BOS	MLB	26	698	134	65.2	.338	-0.1	SS(153): -20.8	4.3
2020	BOS	MLB	27	595	123	41.2	.320	0.9	SS -9	3.4

Xander Bogaerts, continued

Batted Ball Distribution

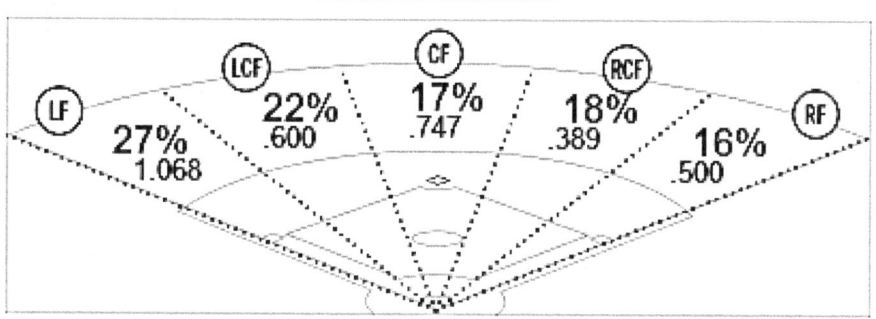

Strike Zone vs LHP   Strike Zone vs RHP

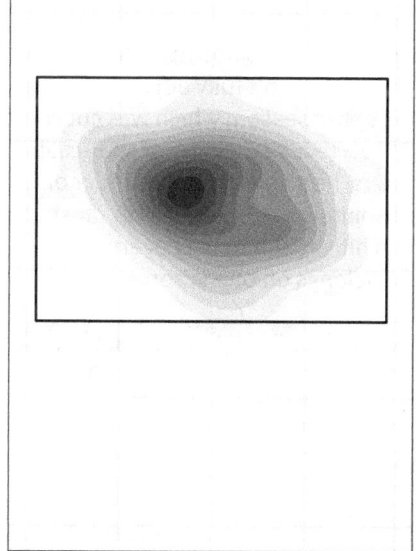

Michael Chavis INF

Born: 08/11/95 Age: 24 Bats: R Throws: R
Height: 5'10" Weight: 216 Origin: Round 1, 2014 Draft (#26 overall)

YEAR	TEAM	LVL	AGE	PA	R	2B	3B	HR	RBI	BB	K	SB	CS	AVG/OBP/SLG
2017	SLM	A+	21	250	50	17	2	17	55	19	57	1	0	.318/.388/.641
2017	PME	AA	21	274	39	18	0	14	39	20	56	1	0	.250/.310/.492
2018	PME	AA	22	139	23	7	0	6	17	13	35	3	1	.303/.388/.508
2018	PAW	AAA	22	34	8	3	0	2	7	1	12	0	0	.273/.294/.545
2019	PAW	AAA	23	79	11	4	0	7	11	8	21	0	0	.257/.329/.614
2019	BOS	MLB	23	382	46	10	1	18	58	31	127	2	1	.254/.322/.444
2020	BOS	MLB	24	595	71	26	1	28	83	45	194	3	1	.237/.303/.446

Comparables: Shed Long, Trevor Story, Jeimer Candelario

For a brief while, it looked like Chavis might save the 2019 Red Sox. Pressed into duty in late April when the Sox were already struggling, the rookie briefly took the league by storm. The short, stocky slugger hit .290/.389/.570 through his first 25 games, providing the club with the type of spark it sorely lacked for a majority of the season. Unfortunately, the league adjusted—primarily by pitching him up and in with hard stuff—and as is often the case with rookies, Chavis couldn't fully adjust back. He hit just .240/.296/.398 for the remainder of his debut season, which was cut short by a sprained AC joint in mid-August. Chavis revealed plenty of MLB-caliber skills, though. He can sock some majestic taters, he's a passable defender on the right side of the infield, and he can absolutely serve as a team's most adorable celebrator, but it's still unclear if he can hit enough to play every day for a first-division team. At least 2019 revealed he belongs on one in some capacity.

YEAR	TEAM	LVL	AGE	PA	DRC+	VORP	BABIP	BRR	FRAA	WARP
2017	SLM	A+	21	250	174	28.2	.360	1.3	3B(27): -1.6	2.4
2017	PME	AA	21	274	103	11.8	.265	0.1	3B(43): -0.5, SS(1): 0.0	0.8
2018	PME	AA	22	139	146	13.3	.383	0.5	3B(18): 1.5, 1B(11): -0.5	1.2
2018	PAW	AAA	22	34	90	4.7	.368	0.2	3B(4): -1.2, 1B(1): 0.0	-0.1
2019	PAW	AAA	23	79	143	8.0	.256	-0.7	3B(7): -0.6, 2B(7): 1.6	0.7
2019	BOS	MLB	23	382	93	5.8	.347	0.0	1B(49): 2.4, 2B(45): -0.9	0.7
2020	BOS	MLB	24	595	96	12.3	.314	0.1	1B 1, 2B 0	1.4

Michael Chavis, continued

Batted Ball Distribution

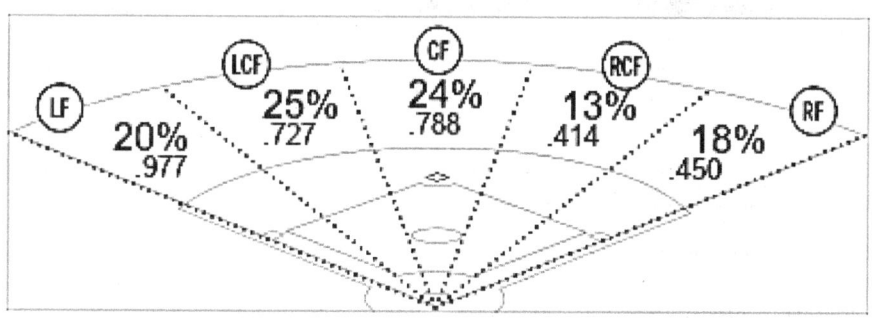

Strike Zone vs LHP   **Strike Zone vs RHP**

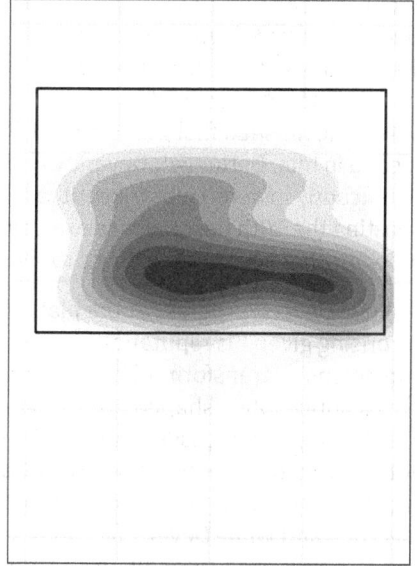

Boston Red Sox 2020

Rafael Devers 3B
Born: 10/24/96   Age: 23   Bats: L   Throws: R
Height: 6'0"   Weight: 237   Origin: International Free Agent, 2013

YEAR	TEAM	LVL	AGE	PA	R	2B	3B	HR	RBI	BB	K	SB	CS	AVG/OBP/SLG
2017	PME	AA	20	320	48	19	3	18	56	31	55	0	3	.300/.369/.575
2017	PAW	AAA	20	38	6	1	0	2	4	3	8	0	0	.400/.447/.600
2017	BOS	MLB	20	240	34	14	0	10	30	18	57	3	1	.284/.338/.482
2018	BOS	MLB	21	490	59	24	0	21	66	38	121	5	2	.240/.298/.433
2019	BOS	MLB	22	702	129	54	4	32	115	48	119	8	8	.311/.361/.555
2020	BOS	MLB	23	595	73	40	2	27	87	41	111	5	2	.278/.332/.505

Comparables: Rougned Odor, Carlos Correa, Gleyber Torres

What were you doing when you were 22? Maybe you took a year off to find yourself. Maybe you headed straight to grad school. Maybe you moved back home for a bit to find your footing. Or maybe you became one of the dozen-or-so best hitters in baseball. No? Guess that's just Devers, then. It's funny to say about someone who's younger than 7th Heaven, but for years now, scouts have hinted at potential greatness in Devers' bat. He'd shown glimpses here and there, but was also prone to months-long stretches where he looked utterly overmatched. Not so in 2019. Devers finished 11th overall in WARP among hitters. He finished first in the majors in total bases, second in doubles and second in hits. Better yet, Devers' dominance looks sustainable, as he significantly lowered his strikeout rate while offering insane plate coverage and boasting the 16th best average exit velocity in the game. The middle-of-the-order masher scouts have long prophesied has arrived.

While Devers' progress at the plate was dramatic, it's perhaps not all that surprising given his reputation and resume. More stunning were the physical and defensive transformations Devers enjoyed. He showed up in spring training with a noticeably reshaped body, improving his conditioning in the hopes of avoiding more soft tissue injuries. He also made tremendous defensive strides at third, and though it's unlikely any Gold Gloves are in his future, he looks capable of manning the hot corner for the next several seasons. Add it all together, and while Devers' face may say "hello I am a harmless baby"—his nickname is Carita, after all—his performance and contract combine to tell a different story: he's now the Red Sox's most valuable player.

YEAR	TEAM	LVL	AGE	PA	DRC+	VORP	BABIP	BRR	FRAA	WARP
2017	PME	AA	20	320	153	26.5	.316	-0.7	3B(64): 4.6	3.3
2017	PAW	AAA	20	38	151	5.5	.480	0.1	3B(8): -2.1	0.1
2017	BOS	MLB	20	240	106	11.6	.342	0.2	3B(56): 4.9	1.6
2018	BOS	MLB	21	490	94	13.3	.281	1.7	3B(116): 11.2	2.8
2019	BOS	MLB	22	702	125	50.0	.339	0.2	3B(152): 7.2, SS(1): 0.0	5.6
2020	*BOS*	*MLB*	*23*	*595*	*112*	*25.1*	*.306*	*1.1*	*3B 8*	*3.4*

Boston Red Sox 2020

Rafael Devers, continued

Batted Ball Distribution

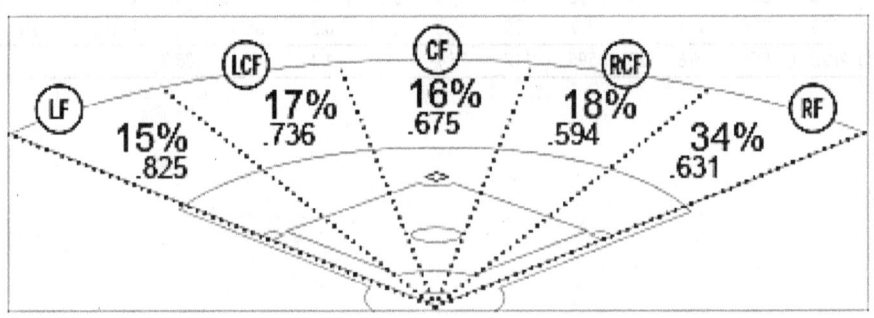

Strike Zone vs LHP   **Strike Zone vs RHP**

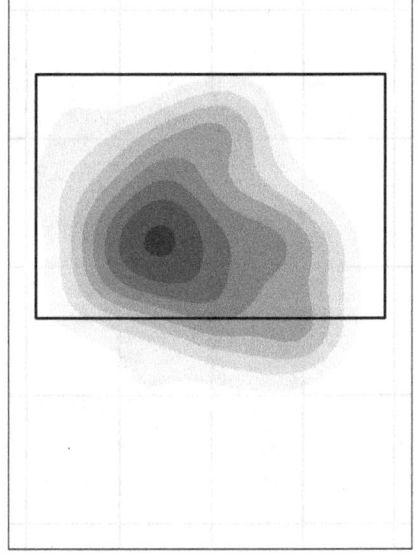

Marco Hernández MI

Born: 09/06/92 Age: 27 Bats: L Throws: R
Height: 6'0" Weight: 200 Origin: International Free Agent, 2009

YEAR	TEAM	LVL	AGE	PA	R	2B	3B	HR	RBI	BB	K	SB	CS	AVG/OBP/SLG
2017	BOS	MLB	24	60	7	3	0	0	2	1	15	0	1	.276/.300/.328
2019	SLM	A+	26	91	15	7	0	0	9	8	9	1	1	.295/.374/.385
2019	PAW	AAA	26	146	23	12	0	2	11	6	32	3	2	.285/.308/.416
2019	BOS	MLB	26	155	18	7	0	2	11	3	42	1	2	.250/.279/.338
2020	BOS	MLB	27	175	15	9	1	3	17	7	43	1	0	.243/.280/.360

Comparables: Charlie Culberson, Danny Santana, Edmundo Sosa

A full 1,112 days: that's how long Hernández went in between his first two major-league home runs. Both came against the same pitcher—Mychal Givens—and both came as Hernández vied for playing time on disappointing Red Sox teams. But while the opponent he victimized and the circumstances he faced were similar, Hernández himself had been through a world of change. After the promising start to his career was cut short by a dislocated shoulder early in 2017, Hernández had to battle through three surgeries to the joint that left him unable to swing consistently for nearly 18 months. It's a real triumph, then, that Hernández looks to be much the same guy we saw way back in 2016; a good hitter against righties who can capably man second base, and who can step in at third or at short in a pinch. Now with a Red Sox team that could potentially lose Brock Holt to free agency and has no real plan at the keystone at present, Hernández's perseverance could land him a significant role.

YEAR	TEAM	LVL	AGE	PA	DRC+	VORP	BABIP	BRR	FRAA	WARP
2017	BOS	MLB	24	60	68	-1.0	.372	-0.3	3B(9): 0.0, 2B(6): 1.7	0.1
2019	SLM	A+	26	91	132	4.4	.324	-1.1	SS(11): -2.3, 2B(6): -1.7	0.0
2019	PAW	AAA	26	146	92	1.1	.349	-0.1	2B(24): 0.3, SS(8): -0.7	0.3
2019	BOS	MLB	26	155	60	-3.0	.337	-0.6	2B(48): 0.1, SS(2): 0.0	-0.3
2020	BOS	MLB	27	175	65	-1.5	.310	0.0	2B -1, 3B 0	-0.2

Boston Red Sox 2020

Marco Hernández, continued

Batted Ball Distribution

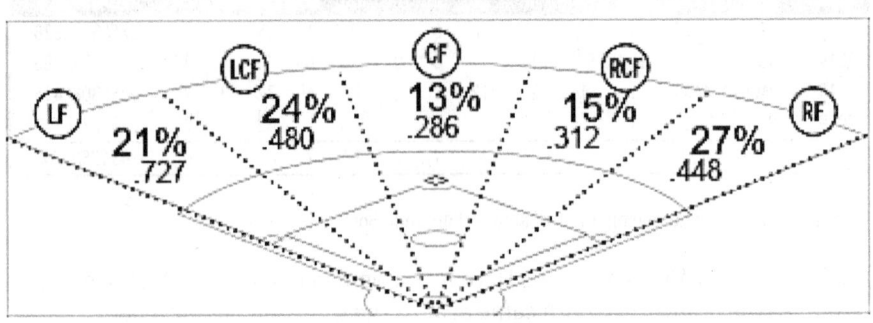

Strike Zone vs LHP   **Strike Zone vs RHP**

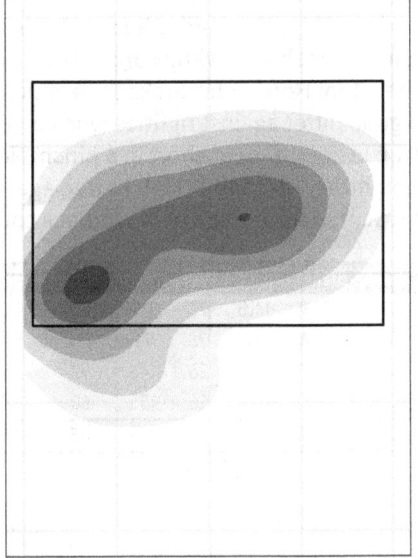

Brock Holt INF

Born: 06/11/88 Age: 32 Bats: L Throws: R
Height: 5'10" Weight: 180 Origin: Round 9, 2009 Draft (#265 overall)

YEAR	TEAM	LVL	AGE	PA	R	2B	3B	HR	RBI	BB	K	SB	CS	AVG/OBP/SLG
2017	PAW	AAA	29	77	9	1	0	3	9	6	14	0	0	.214/.286/.357
2017	BOS	MLB	29	164	20	6	0	0	7	19	34	2	1	.200/.305/.243
2018	BOS	MLB	30	367	41	18	2	7	46	37	73	7	7	.277/.362/.411
2019	PAW	AAA	31	37	7	2	0	1	3	8	12	1	0	.250/.432/.429
2019	BOS	MLB	31	295	38	14	2	3	31	28	57	1	0	.297/.369/.402
2020	BOS	MLB	32	251	25	11	1	4	24	24	54	4	2	.254/.335/.368

Comparables: Josh Harrison, Hubie Brooks, Matt Tolbert

On the surface, Holt might just appear as a decent utility player who's getting a bit long in the tooth. But to the Red Sox, Holt has been much more than that. He was the only thing that made them watchable way back in 2015. He hit for the cycle against the dreaded Yankees in the 2018 ALCS. He's huge in the Boston philanthropy scene. And he's Andrew Benintendi's sidekick. Holt's free agency, then, should provide an interesting litmus test for new Chief Baseball Officer Chaim Bloom. Will Bloom and company throw a few million Holt's way to ensure he keeps serving as the organization's safety blanket, potentially earning a few points with Red Sox fans along the way? Or will value dictate that some combination of Marco Hernández, Tzu-Wei Lin and C.J. Chatham can take his job on the cheap? If Bloom picks door number two, expect the loss of Holt to hit Sox fans a lot harder than you'd think it ought to.

YEAR	TEAM	LVL	AGE	PA	DRC+	VORP	BABIP	BRR	FRAA	WARP
2017	PAW	AAA	29	77	82	0.5	.226	0.1	LF(7): 1.3, 3B(4): 0.1	0.2
2017	BOS	MLB	29	164	69	-3.1	.259	0.6	2B(31): 0.1, LF(10): 0.7	0.0
2018	BOS	MLB	30	367	101	13.4	.337	-1.9	2B(56): -5.3, SS(23): -2.0	0.1
2019	PAW	AAA	31	37	108	2.8	.400	0.0	SS(3): 1.1, 2B(2): -0.3	0.2
2019	BOS	MLB	31	295	98	8.6	.365	-1.1	2B(60): 3.7, 1B(11): 1.7	1.3
2020	BOS	MLB	32	251	89	4.5	.317	-0.2	2B 0, SS 0	0.5

Boston Red Sox 2020

Brock Holt, continued

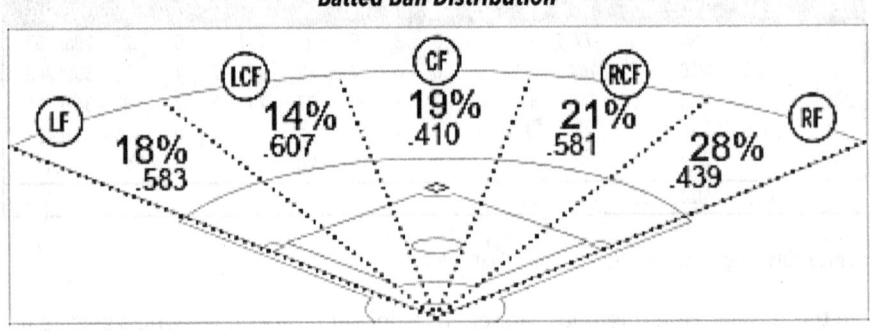

Batted Ball Distribution

Strike Zone vs LHP		Strike Zone vs RHP

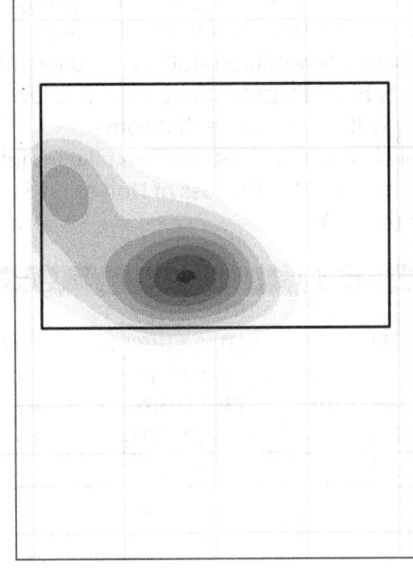 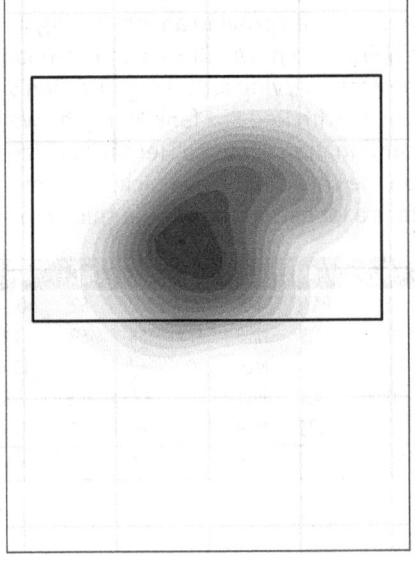

Jonathan Lucroy C

Born: 06/13/86　Age: 34　Bats: R　Throws: R
Height: 6'0"　Weight: 200　Origin: Round 3, 2007 Draft (#101 overall)

YEAR	TEAM	LVL	AGE	PA	R	2B	3B	HR	RBI	BB	K	SB	CS	AVG/OBP/SLG
2017	TEX	MLB	31	306	27	15	0	4	27	19	32	1	0	.242/.297/.338
2017	COL	MLB	31	175	18	6	3	2	13	27	19	0	0	.310/.429/.437
2018	OAK	MLB	32	454	41	21	1	4	51	29	65	0	0	.241/.291/.325
2019	CHN	MLB	33	60	2	2	0	1	6	6	12	0	0	.189/.283/.283
2019	LAA	MLB	33	268	28	8	1	7	30	21	39	0	0	.242/.310/.371
2020	CHN	MLB	34	251	25	11	1	6	26	22	42	1	0	.242/.315/.375

Comparables: Don Slaught, Damon Berryhill, Brian Schneider

It's remarkable how quickly things fell apart for Lucroy. He was the best hitting catcher in baseball in 2014, and even finished fourth in NL MVP voting due to his contributions at the dish and behind it. In 2016, he was a hot commodity at the trade deadline for the same reasons. And, in the years since? His bat has been downright offensive as he's lost power and no longer is a big enough threat to draw walks. Lucroy keeps cashing checks due to a defensive reputation that our metrics suggest he no longer merits, and he figures to hang around for at least a couple more seasons as a backup. But Lord, it appears his days as a meaningful contributor are here, and far sooner than expected.

YEAR	TEAM	P. COUNT	FRM RUNS	BLK RUNS	THRW RUNS	TOT RUNS
2017	TEX	9640	-11.1	-1.2	0.6	-12.2
2017	COL	5958	-6.8	-1.8	0.1	-8.8
2018	OAK	16900	-3.7	-3.7	0.3	-7.3
2019	LAA	9556	-3.1	-5.5	0.4	-8.4
2019	CHN	2272	-0.7	0.0	-0.2	-1.0
2020	CHN	12446	-4.9	-2.0	0.4	-6.5

YEAR	TEAM	LVL	AGE	PA	DRC+	VORP	BABIP	BRR	FRAA	WARP
2017	TEX	MLB	31	306	95	0.1	.259	1.0	C(66): -0.7, 1B(1): 0.0	1.2
2017	COL	MLB	31	175	93	13.4	.341	-0.2	C(44): 0.6	0.8
2018	OAK	MLB	32	454	82	2.2	.273	-2.5	C(125): -9.7	0.0
2019	CHN	MLB	33	60	65	0.3	.225	-0.5	C(20): 0.4, 1B(4): 0.0	0.0
2019	LAA	MLB	33	268	88	9.5	.259	-2.5		-0.2
2020	CHN	MLB	34	251	85	2.3	.274	-0.7	C -7, 1B 0	-0.5

Boston Red Sox 2020

Jonathan Lucroy, continued

Batted Ball Distribution

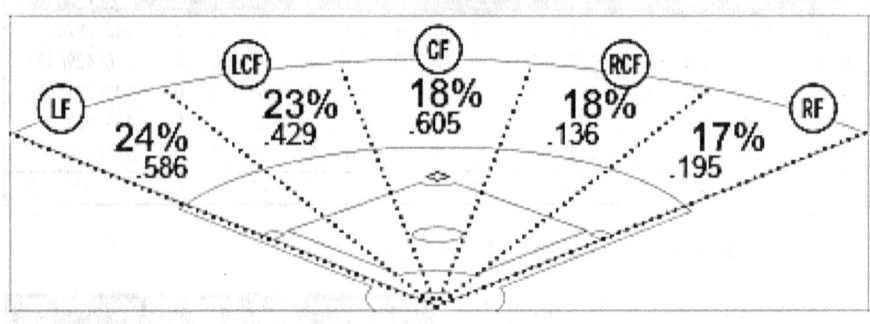

Strike Zone vs LHP   **Strike Zone vs RHP**

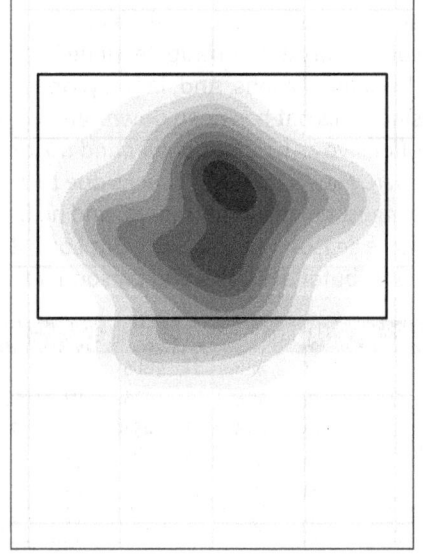

J.D. Martinez DH

Born: 08/21/87 Age: 32 Bats: R Throws: R
Height: 6'3" Weight: 220 Origin: Round 20, 2009 Draft (#611 overall)

YEAR	TEAM	LVL	AGE	PA	R	2B	3B	HR	RBI	BB	K	SB	CS	AVG/OBP/SLG
2017	DET	MLB	29	232	38	13	2	16	39	29	54	2	0	.305/.388/.630
2017	ARI	MLB	29	257	47	13	1	29	65	24	74	2	0	.302/.366/.741
2018	BOS	MLB	30	649	111	37	2	43	130	69	146	6	1	.330/.402/.629
2019	BOS	MLB	31	657	98	33	2	36	105	72	138	2	0	.304/.383/.557
2020	BOS	MLB	32	630	90	37	2	37	105	63	150	4	2	.290/.365/.555

Comparables: Cliff Floyd, Geoff Jenkins, Ryan Braun

In Martinez's 2019 *Annual* comment, we remarked that giving the best players a lot of money leads to good results. Yet a popular narrative in Boston this offseason centered on how Martinez handicapped the suddenly cost-conscious Red Sox by declining to opt out of his contract. In many ways, that's ridiculous. While Martinez took a slight step back from his otherworldly 2018 campaign, he still paced the Sox in slugging percentage, homers and DRC+. Per WARP, he was one of the best 30-or-so hitters in the game. Any offense would be lucky to have him. And yet, there's an argument to be made that he no longer represents Boston's best allocation of resources, given their self-imposed financial bind. Mookie Betts, Xander Bogaerts and Rafael Devers all provided more offensive value while also playing important positions in the field, and for all of the Red Sox's woes last season, they finished fourth in team DRC+. It's wildly unfair that Martinez can be one of the 20-or-so most feared hitters on the planet, make just $22 million a year and be viewed as a liability rather than an asset, but welcome to how the owners have conditioned many to think in 2020. Don't fall for it; Martinez remains a stud.

YEAR	TEAM	LVL	AGE	PA	DRC+	VORP	BABIP	BRR	FRAA	WARP
2017	DET	MLB	29	232	162	18.3	.338	-1.5	RF(53): -6.3	1.5
2017	ARI	MLB	29	257	158	26.4	.315	-2.4	RF(60): -3.9	1.8
2018	BOS	MLB	30	649	167	57.2	.375	-3.9	LF(32): -0.9, RF(25): 2.4	6.3
2019	BOS	MLB	31	657	139	45.3	.342	-6.2	RF(24): 3.8, LF(15): 0.5	4.2
2020	BOS	MLB	32	630	140	38.3	.337	-4.6	LF -1, RF 0	3.9

J.D. Martinez, continued

Batted Ball Distribution

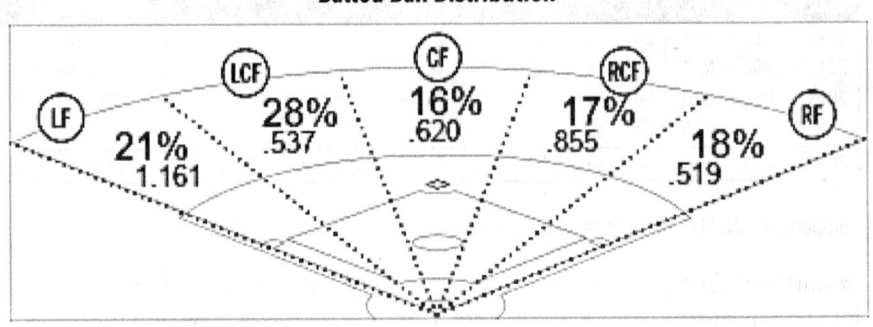

Strike Zone vs LHP

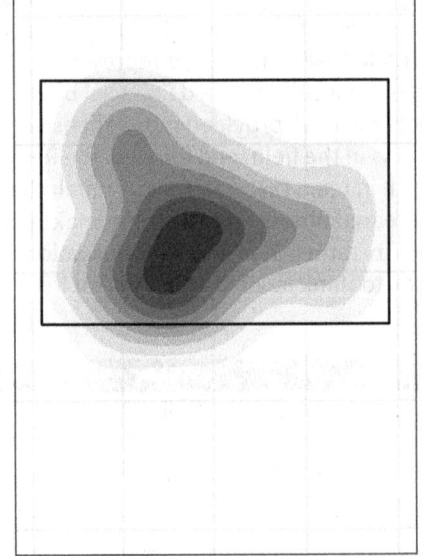

Strike Zone vs RHP

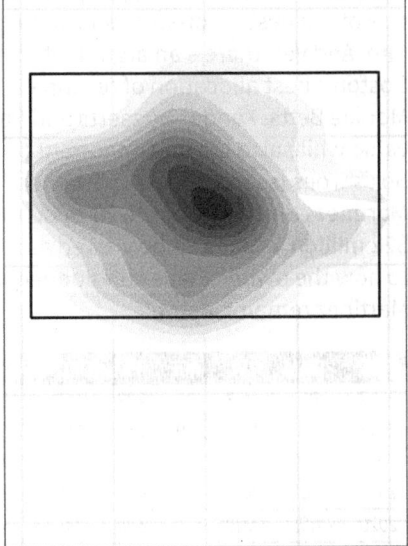

Mitch Moreland   1B

Born: 09/06/85   Age: 34   Bats: L   Throws: L
Height: 6'2"   Weight: 230   Origin: Round 17, 2007 Draft (#530 overall)

YEAR	TEAM	LVL	AGE	PA	R	2B	3B	HR	RBI	BB	K	SB	CS	AVG/OBP/SLG
2017	BOS	MLB	31	576	73	34	0	22	79	57	120	0	1	.246/.326/.443
2018	BOS	MLB	32	459	57	23	4	15	68	50	102	2	0	.245/.325/.433
2019	BOS	MLB	33	335	48	17	1	19	58	34	74	1	0	.252/.328/.507
2020	BOS	MLB	34	350	40	15	1	15	45	32	86	1	0	.225/.301/.416

Comparables: Eric Hinske, Adam LaRoche, Derrek Lee

On a rate basis, Moreland was actually better last season than he was in 2018, when he played a complementary but important role on the World Series champs. The problem in 2019 was that Moreland spent nearly as much time hurt as he did on the diamond. The lumbering lefty struggled with back and quad injuries en route to appearing in his fewest games in a season since 2014, which was bad news for a Sox squad forced to start all sorts of riffraff at first base during his absence. Though his ceiling is lower than a priest hole's, Moreland still has some value to offer on a one-year contract as a platoon bat and capable defender at first base. Unfortunately, he exists in a timeline in which half the orgs in baseball would rather be cheap than good.

YEAR	TEAM	LVL	AGE	PA	DRC+	VORP	BABIP	BRR	FRAA	WARP
2017	BOS	MLB	31	576	103	3.3	.278	-2.7	1B(138): 5.7, P(1): 0.0	1.3
2018	BOS	MLB	32	459	103	3.4	.288	-2.5	1B(116): 2.4	0.8
2019	BOS	MLB	33	335	111	10.3	.271	-2.6	1B(85): 4.3	1.2
2020	BOS	MLB	34	350	88	3.0	.262	-1.6	1B 2	0.7

Mitch Moreland, continued

Batted Ball Distribution

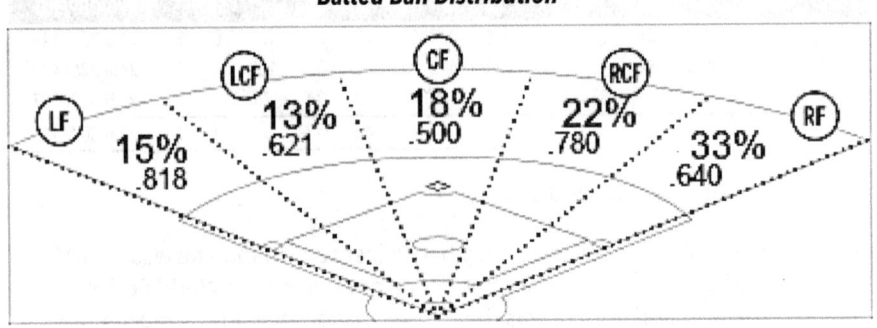

Strike Zone vs LHP

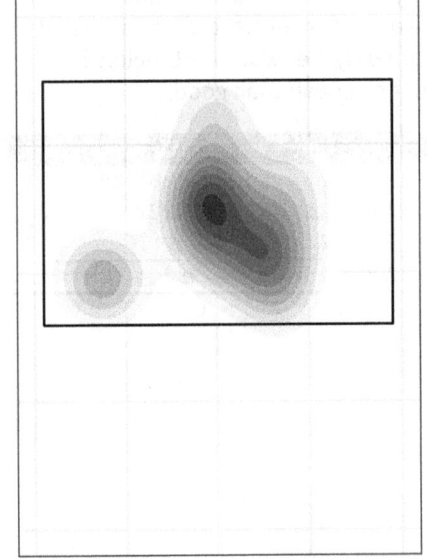

Strike Zone vs RHP

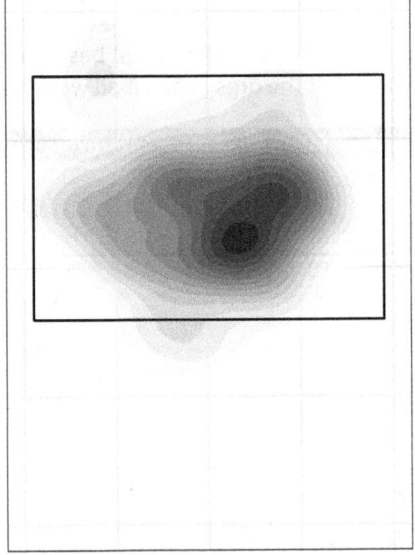

Steve Pearce 1B

Born: 04/13/83   Age: 37   Bats: R   Throws: R
Height: 5'11"   Weight: 200   Origin: Round 8, 2005 Draft (#241 overall)

YEAR	TEAM	LVL	AGE	PA	R	2B	3B	HR	RBI	BB	K	SB	CS	AVG/OBP/SLG
2017	TOR	MLB	34	348	38	17	1	13	37	27	68	0	0	.252/.319/.438
2018	TOR	MLB	35	86	16	6	0	4	16	7	14	0	0	.291/.349/.519
2018	BOS	MLB	35	165	19	8	1	7	26	22	27	0	0	.279/.394/.507
2019	PAW	AAA	36	29	3	1	0	0	2	3	10	0	0	.167/.310/.208
2019	BOS	MLB	36	99	9	4	0	1	9	7	31	0	0	.180/.245/.258
2020	BOS	MLB	37	251	27	12	1	9	30	22	69	1	0	.234/.312/.411

Comparables: Brian Giles, Dwight Evans, Shin-Soo Choo

"The Patriot Way" is code for lots of things—image rehabilitation, disdain for the media, the dehumanization of players, etc—but one of its more useful tenets is that it's better to get out on a dude a year too early than a year too late. With Pearce, it looks like the Sox should have borrowed their football brethren's playbook. Sure, you can understand why the Boston brass wanted a reunion with the reigning World Series MVP. He only cost $6.25 million, he made a good platoon partner with Mitch Moreland on paper and did we mention that he'd just improbably won World Series MVP? Then again, the Sox likely outbid themselves for a 36-year-old short-side platoon bat's services, and Pearce was unable to reward their loyalty. A miserable start gave way to a back injury that put him on the IL, and while rehabbing that particular booboo, he partially tore his PCL. Hindsight is 20/20 and all that, but it looks like Pearce missed his chance to go out a conquering hero, and is instead headed toward a less distinguished end.

YEAR	TEAM	LVL	AGE	PA	DRC+	VORP	BABIP	BRR	FRAA	WARP
2017	TOR	MLB	34	348	100	7.5	.281	0.3	LF(85): 3.3, 1B(10): -0.4	1.2
2018	TOR	MLB	35	86	130	5.1	.311	0.7	LF(9): -1.4, 1B(3): 0.4	0.5
2018	BOS	MLB	35	165	133	10.6	.298	-1.4	1B(31): -1.0, LF(2): -0.1	0.7
2019	PAW	AAA	36	29	68	-0.3	.286	0.3	1B(4): 1.0	0.0
2019	BOS	MLB	36	99	60	-3.3	.259	-0.3	1B(19): 0.9, LF(4): 0.6	-0.2
2020	BOS	MLB	37	251	91	5.0	.297	-0.2	LF 1, 1B 0	0.7

Boston Red Sox 2020

Steve Pearce, continued

Batted Ball Distribution

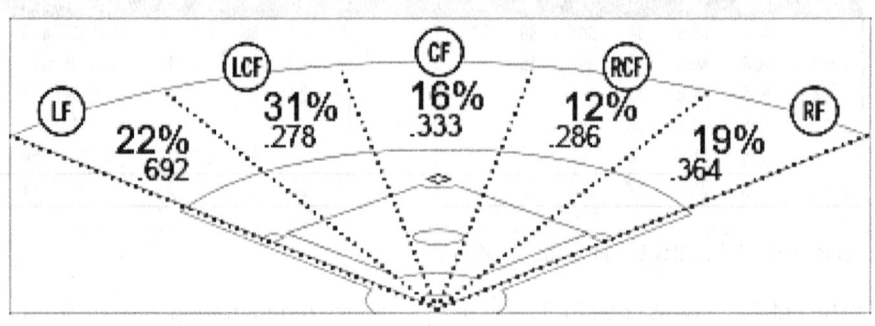

Strike Zone vs LHP   **Strike Zone vs RHP**

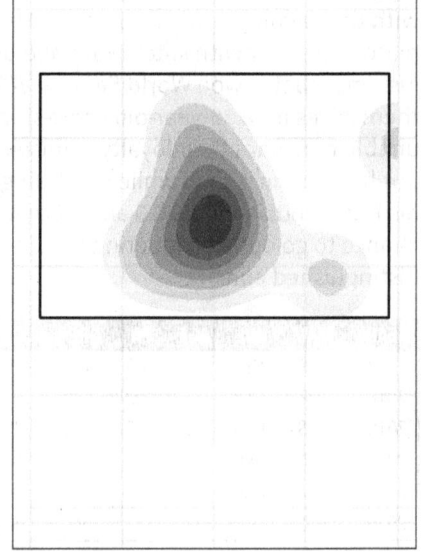

José Peraza UT

Born: 04/30/94 Age: 26 Bats: R Throws: R
Height: 6'0" Weight: 196 Origin: International Free Agent, 2010

YEAR	TEAM	LVL	AGE	PA	R	2B	3B	HR	RBI	BB	K	SB	CS	AVG/OBP/SLG
2017	CIN	MLB	23	518	50	9	4	5	37	20	70	23	8	.259/.297/.324
2018	CIN	MLB	24	683	85	31	4	14	58	29	75	23	6	.288/.326/.416
2019	CIN	MLB	25	403	37	18	2	6	33	17	58	7	6	.239/.285/.346
2020	BOS	MLB	26	350	32	16	2	6	33	15	51	14	5	.255/.295/.367

Comparables: Donovan Solano, Jose Lopez, José Altuve

Peraza's at-bats should be sponsored by Bumble because the intention for each is to connect with a single. He doesn't walk, he doesn't bop and he didn't even steal efficiently (or often) last season. If we didn't know any better, we'd say he was auditioning for a gig with the Royals. First, though, he'll take a tour of Boston. Peraza will turn 26 in April, meaning he's likely to get at least a few more chances to live up to his old promise and/or replicate his solid 2018. He won't; not unless he hits .280 or better.

YEAR	TEAM	LVL	AGE	PA	DRC+	VORP	BABIP	BRR	FRAA	WARP
2017	CIN	MLB	23	518	76	-0.4	.293	0.6	2B(77): 2.3, SS(55): 0.6	0.7
2018	CIN	MLB	24	683	101	31.7	.307	2.4	SS(156): -3.4, RF(1): 0.0	3.1
2019	CIN	MLB	25	403	79	3.8	.268	2.7	2B(78): 1.0, SS(39): 0.3	0.5
2020	BOS	MLB	26	350	75	3.1	.287	0.8	2B 2, LF 0	0.5

José Peraza, continued

Batted Ball Distribution

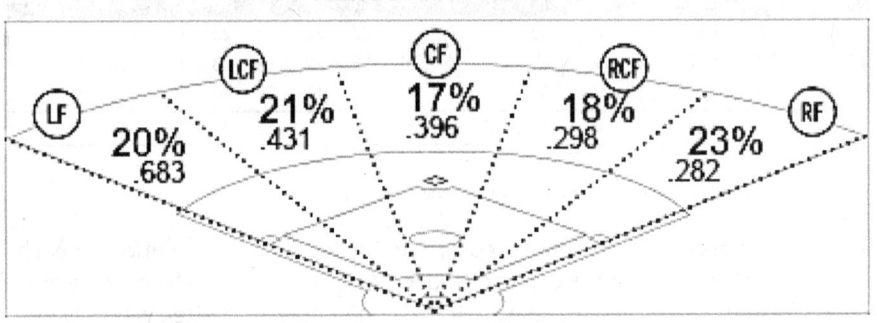

Strike Zone vs LHP **Strike Zone vs RHP**

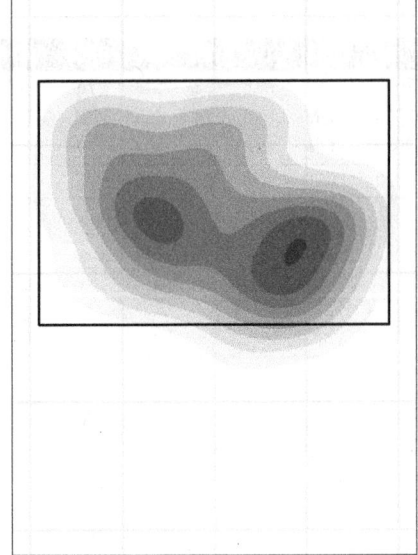

Kevin Pillar CF

Born: 01/04/89   Age: 31   Bats: R   Throws: R
Height: 6'0"   Weight: 210   Origin: Round 32, 2011 Draft (#979 overall)

YEAR	TEAM	LVL	AGE	PA	R	2B	3B	HR	RBI	BB	K	SB	CS	AVG/OBP/SLG
2017	TOR	MLB	28	632	72	37	1	16	42	33	95	15	6	.256/.300/.404
2018	TOR	MLB	29	542	65	40	2	15	59	18	98	14	3	.252/.282/.426
2019	TOR	MLB	30	17	1	0	0	0	1	0	3	0	0	.063/.059/.063
2019	SFN	MLB	30	628	82	37	3	21	87	18	86	14	5	.264/.293/.442
2020	*SFN*	*MLB*	*31*	*400*	*36*	*21*	*1*	*9*	*41*	*16*	*61*	*10*	*3*	*.239/.278/.370*

Comparables: Daniel Murphy, Elston Howard, Gerardo Parra

On November 14th, 2019, it was revealed that San Francisco baseball writer Hank Schulman awarded Pillar with a 10th-place MVP vote, the first of his career. Was it possible that after Pillar's trade across leagues in early April, he could've posted a career year and emerged as one of the ten best players in his new league? Of course! After all, he had a reputation for stellar defense in center field, and enough power to light up scoreboards if he could ever resist the urge to swing at pitches outside the zone.

But that wasn't what *actually* happened in Pillar's sixth full major-league season. Yes, he only missed a fistful of games as the linchpin of San Francisco's mix-and-match outfield, but his once-lauded defense in center fell apart completely, and he provided negative offensive value thanks to his distressing .287 OBP (only surpassed in the race for the bottom by former teammate Randal Grichuk). His aggressiveness—he had the highest swing rate on pitches outside the zone and third-highest swing rate overall—works for elite bat-to-ball guys like Nick Castellanos and Jeff McNeil, but for Pillar it only resulted in him making outs 70 percent of the time. Alas, Pillar ended up outside even the 10 most valuable Giants position players for the 2019 season, and was non-tendered just weeks after the highest awards honor of his career.

YEAR	TEAM	LVL	AGE	PA	DRC+	VORP	BABIP	BRR	FRAA	WARP
2017	TOR	MLB	28	632	87	8.0	.280	-1.1	CF(153): -6.2	0.5
2018	TOR	MLB	29	542	94	16.1	.281	3.3	CF(142): 9.0	2.8
2019	TOR	MLB	30	17	27	-0.7	.071	0.0	CF(4): 0.1	-0.1
2019	SFN	MLB	30	628	87	10.9	.275	4.1	CF(129): -10.8, RF(27): 0.2	0.4
2020	*SFN*	*MLB*	*31*	*400*	*73*	*-0.2*	*.264*	*1.0*	*CF -1, RF 0*	*-0.2*

Kevin Pillar, continued

Batted Ball Distribution

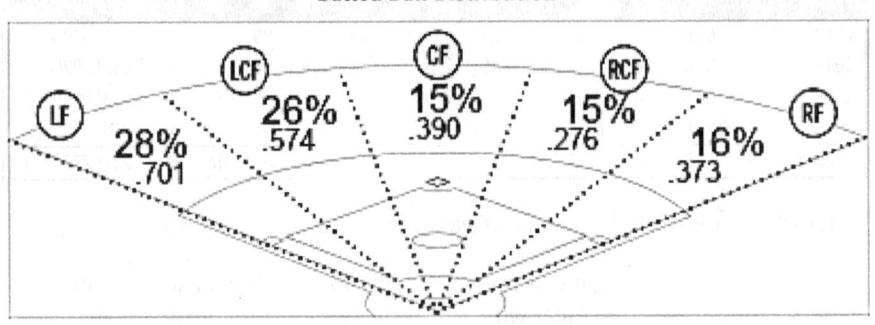

Strike Zone vs LHP   **Strike Zone vs RHP**

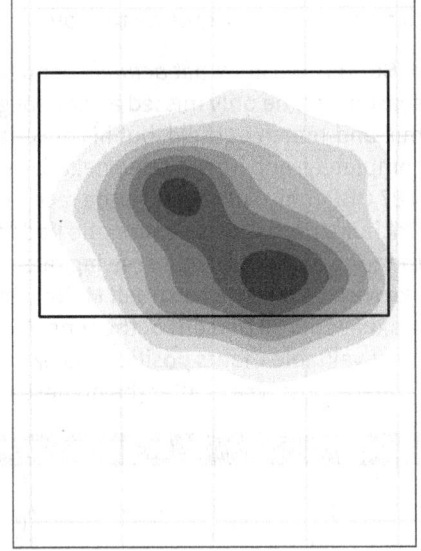

Kevin Plawecki C

Born: 02/26/91 Age: 29 Bats: R Throws: R
Height: 6'2" Weight: 220 Origin: Round 1, 2012 Draft (#35 overall)

YEAR	TEAM	LVL	AGE	PA	R	2B	3B	HR	RBI	BB	K	SB	CS	AVG/OBP/SLG
2017	LVG	AAA	26	275	37	17	1	9	45	16	38	0	0	.328/.375/.514
2017	NYN	MLB	26	118	11	5	0	3	13	14	17	1	0	.260/.364/.400
2018	NYN	MLB	27	277	33	13	2	7	30	28	65	0	1	.210/.315/.370
2019	CLE	MLB	28	174	13	10	0	3	17	12	31	0	1	.222/.287/.342
2020	BOS	MLB	29	140	13	6	0	3	14	11	29	0	0	.215/.289/.346

Comparables: Hank Conger, Derek Norris, Andy Etchebarren

YEAR	TEAM	P. COUNT	FRM RUNS	BLK RUNS	THRW RUNS	TOT RUNS
2017	LVG	9115	8.7	0.8	-0.4	8.6
2017	NYN	3842	-3.2	0.7	-0.6	-3.3
2018	NYN	9839	-4.6	2.0	0.0	-2.7
2019	CLE	6773	6.6	2.2	-0.3	8.4
2020	BOS	6352	3.2	0.9	-0.3	3.8

When you're coming up in an organization that has a fancier catching prospect, sometimes opportunities can be limited. Plawecki found that out the hard way during his time alongside Travis d'Arnaud in the Mets system. Traded to Cleveland over the winter, he looked in line to replace Yan Gomes. Yet, Plawecki once again disappointed, serving as the backup behind the dish to Roberto Perez and struggling to crack a .600 OPS. His defensive numbers rebounded, per our metrics, but that's the formula for a dependable backup, not someone who deserves a greater opportunity.

YEAR	TEAM	LVL	AGE	PA	DRC+	VORP	BABIP	BRR	FRAA	WARP
2017	LVG	AAA	26	275	125	22.9	.350	-1.4	C(63): 10.7	3.1
2017	NYN	MLB	26	118	101	8.5	.284	-0.3	C(29): -3.3, 1B(2): 0.0	0.2
2018	NYN	MLB	27	277	92	11.5	.257	-1.2	C(71): -2.0, 1B(3): 0.0	0.8
2019	CLE	MLB	28	174	79	4.5	.256	-1.3	C(57): 7.8, P(2): 0.0	1.1
2020	BOS	MLB	29	140	71	0.9	.253	-0.3	C 4	0.5

Boston Red Sox 2020

Kevin Plawecki, continued

Batted Ball Distribution

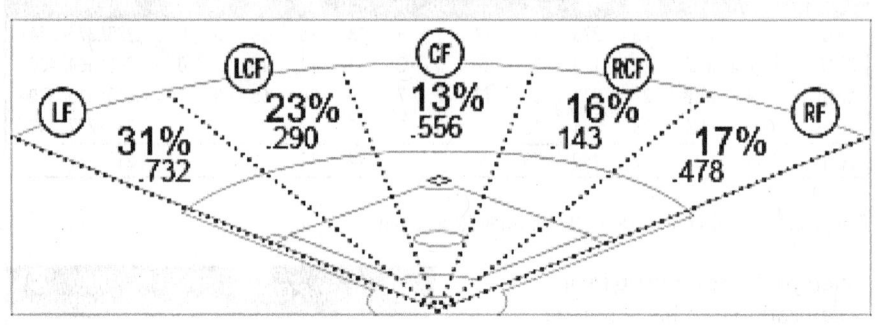

Strike Zone vs LHP   **Strike Zone vs RHP**

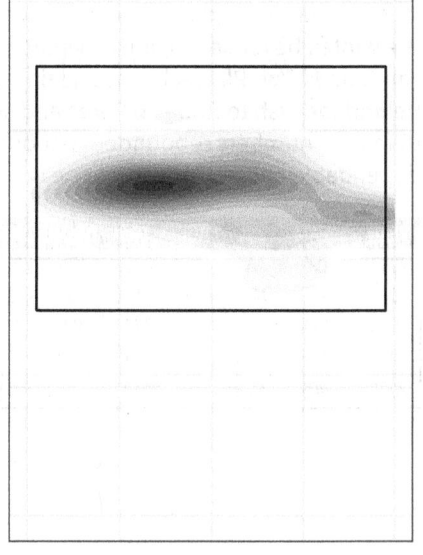

Alex Verdugo OF

Born: 05/15/96   Age: 24   Bats: L   Throws: L
Height: 6'0"   Weight: 212   Origin: Round 2, 2014 Draft (#62 overall)

YEAR	TEAM	LVL	AGE	PA	R	2B	3B	HR	RBI	BB	K	SB	CS	AVG/OBP/SLG
2017	OKL	AAA	21	495	67	27	4	6	62	52	50	9	3	.314/.389/.436
2017	LAN	MLB	21	25	1	0	0	1	1	2	4	0	1	.174/.240/.304
2018	OKL	AAA	22	379	44	19	0	10	44	34	47	8	2	.329/.391/.472
2018	LAN	MLB	22	86	11	6	0	1	4	8	14	0	0	.260/.329/.377
2019	LAN	MLB	23	377	43	22	2	12	44	26	49	4	1	.294/.342/.475
2020	LAN	MLB	24	504	55	24	1	15	59	38	73	4	2	.263/.324/.419

Comparables: Paul Konerko, Joe Torre, Jose Tabata

For most other teams, Verdugo would've been given a shot to start two years ago, but only this past offseason did the Dodgers clear enough of their outfield logjam to give him a spot on the Opening Day roster. He took immediate advantage, posting an .817 OPS along with plus defense in the outfield, playing at a borderline All-Star level while healthy. Not many rookies have the ability to accomplish that, so it was a surprise that he became a bit of a forgotten man down the stretch following the oblique and back injuries that put him out of sight as the Dodgers rolled to 106 wins. Unfortunately, his importance came back to prominence in a hurry in the postseason when he wasn't around to supplant A.J. Pollock, and his bat-to-ball skills were especially missed as Dodger after Dodger struck out in crucial situations. Barring a trade, Verdugo will compete for a job with Pollock in 2020 and, despite the latter's contract, there's no reason Verdugo shouldn't find plenty of playing time available to him.

YEAR	TEAM	LVL	AGE	PA	DRC+	VORP	BABIP	BRR	FRAA	WARP
2017	OKL	AAA	21	495	113	31.4	.340	3.1	CF(59): -5.5, RF(46): 3.1	2.3
2017	LAN	MLB	21	25	86	-1.2	.167	-0.1	CF(6): -0.7, RF(3): 0.0	0.0
2018	OKL	AAA	22	379	128	24.0	.359	-0.5	CF(45): 2.0, RF(31): 2.4	2.8
2018	LAN	MLB	22	86	85	3.3	.306	1.5	RF(16): -0.1, LF(12): 0.2	0.1
2019	LAN	MLB	23	377	102	13.7	.309	1.4	CF(61): -1.2, RF(25): 1.2	1.7
2020	LAN	MLB	24	504	96	10.7	.284	1.8	RF 9, CF 0	1.9

Boston Red Sox 2020

Alex Verdugo, continued

Batted Ball Distribution

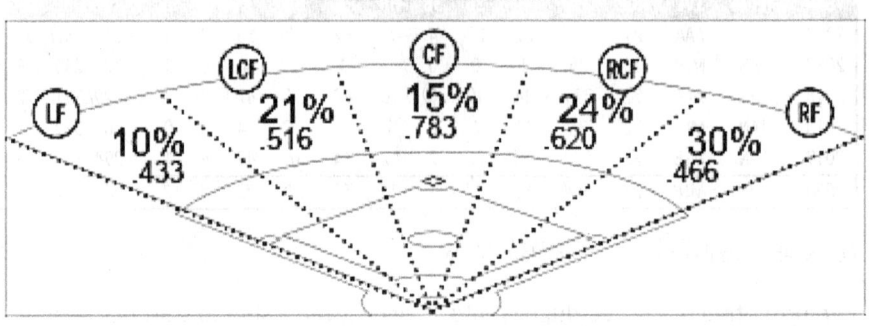

Strike Zone vs LHP   **Strike Zone vs RHP**

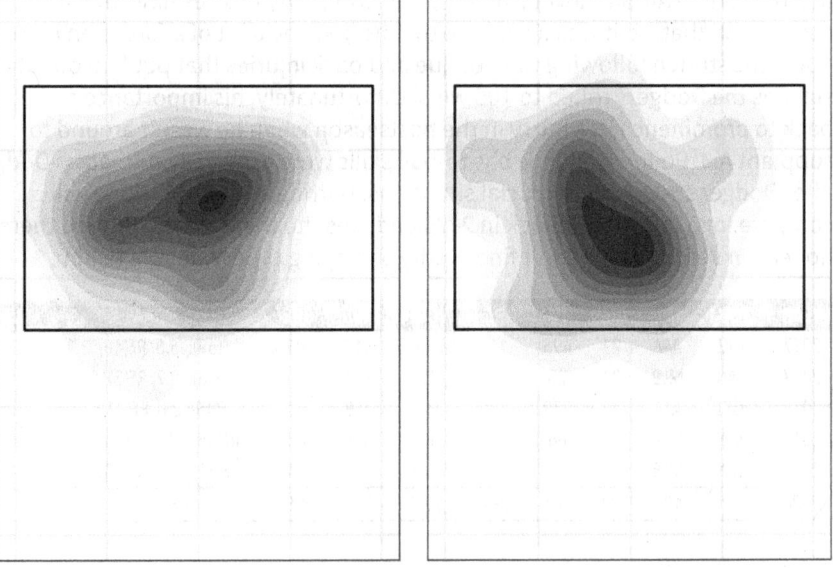

Christian Vázquez C

Born: 08/21/90 Age: 29 Bats: R Throws: R
Height: 5'9" Weight: 195 Origin: Round 9, 2008 Draft (#292 overall)

YEAR	TEAM	LVL	AGE	PA	R	2B	3B	HR	RBI	BB	K	SB	CS	AVG/OBP/SLG
2017	BOS	MLB	26	345	43	18	2	5	32	17	64	7	2	.290/.330/.404
2018	BOS	MLB	27	269	24	10	0	3	16	13	41	4	1	.207/.257/.283
2019	BOS	MLB	28	521	66	26	1	23	72	33	101	4	2	.276/.320/.477
2020	BOS	MLB	29	560	56	26	1	16	62	36	115	6	2	.246/.299/.390

Comparables: Tom Pagnozzi, Brent Mayne, Francisco Cervelli

One season after producing less offensive value than peers like Chris Iannetta, Manny Piña and Austin Romine, Vázquez outhit Buster Posey, Gary Sánchez and Yadier Molina. He hit the ball harder, struck out and walked more, rode some positive BABIP regression and was likely helped quite a bit by the bouncy balls. Vázquez's emergence as an offensive threat is well-timed, because he's trending from elite to merely very good as a defender; one that figures to continue as he enters his 30s. That being said, what he's losing in catching prowess he may learn to compensate for in defensive versatility. In an effort to keep Vázquez's bat in the lineup—a sentence that we can't believe we're typing either—the Red Sox gave him some major-league reps at first, second, third, and yes, even DH. Essentially, this is a drawn-out way of telling you Vázquez has become the player we all though Blake Swihart would be. Catchers, man.

YEAR	TEAM	P. COUNT	FRM RUNS	BLK RUNS	THRW RUNS	TOT RUNS
2017	BOS	13558	15.5	1.0	2.4	19.6
2018	BOS	10330	9.0	0.1	0.1	9.0
2019	BOS	16455	12.3	-5.3	0.8	7.7
2020	BOS	23520	18.5	-2.6	1.6	17.4

YEAR	TEAM	LVL	AGE	PA	DRC+	VORP	BABIP	BRR	FRAA	WARP
2017	BOS	MLB	26	345	93	6.7	.348	-3.3	C(95): 16.4, 3B(2): 0.0	2.7
2018	BOS	MLB	27	269	71	-5.4	.237	-0.4	C(75): 8.3, 3B(2): 0.0	1.2
2019	BOS	MLB	28	521	106	28.3	.305	-0.3	C(119): 7.0, 1B(10): 1.0	3.5
2020	BOS	MLB	29	560	82	10.6	.289	-1.7	C 16, 1B 0	2.7

Christian Vázquez, continued

Batted Ball Distribution

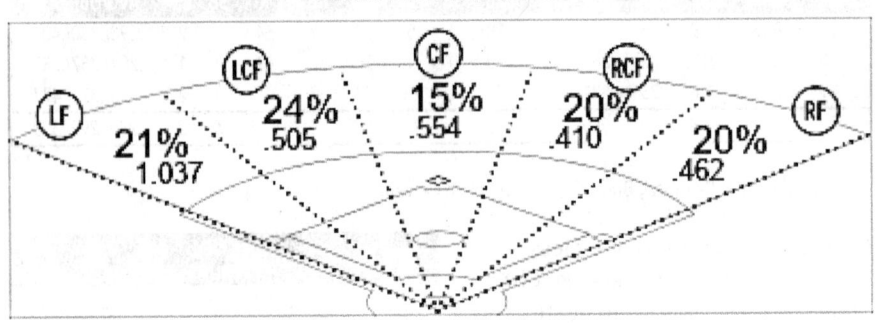

Strike Zone vs LHP   **Strike Zone vs RHP**

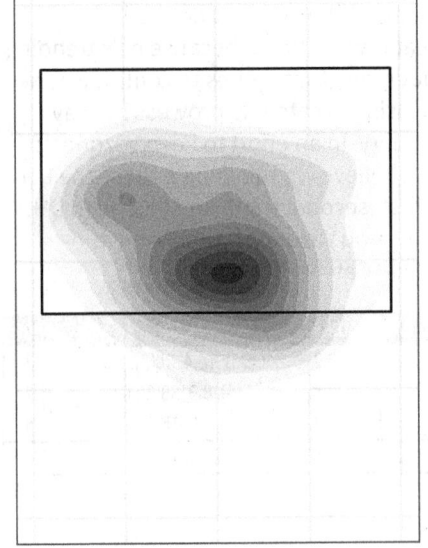 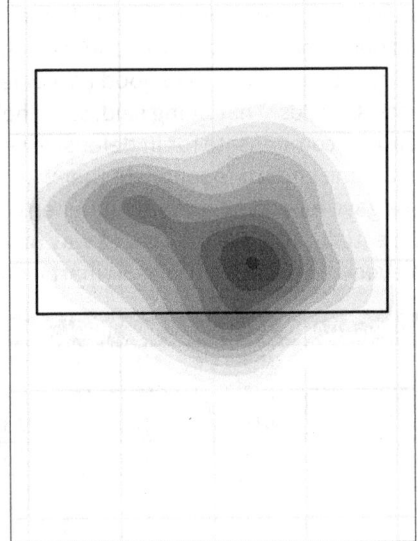

Matt Barnes RHP

Born: 06/17/90   Age: 30   Bats: R   Throws: R
Height: 6'4"   Weight: 210   Origin: Round 1, 2011 Draft (#19 overall)

YEAR	TEAM	LVL	AGE	W	L	SV	G	GS	IP	H	HR	BB/9	K/9	K	GB%	BABIP
2017	BOS	MLB	27	7	3	1	70	0	69^2	57	7	3.6	10.7	83	50%	.298
2018	BOS	MLB	28	6	4	0	62	0	61^2	47	5	4.5	14.0	96	53%	.321
2019	BOS	MLB	29	5	4	4	70	0	64^1	51	8	5.3	15.4	110	48%	.341
2020	BOS	MLB	30	3	3	11	61	0	65	53	7	4.8	13.8	99	49%	.333

Comparables: Cody Martin, Justin Grimm, Tommy Kahnle

For better and for worse, nothing about Barnes' 2019 can be considered surprising. He missed a ton of bats; among pitchers with at least 50 innings he ranked second in the league in K/9 behind only Josh Hader. He also walked too many—he had the 14th worst BB/9 in baseball—and gave up his fair share of taters. That's Barnes in a nutshell, a fireman who's equally as capable of shutting down the heart of an order as he is walking the opposing team's pitcher or serving up a spicy meatball to, like, Bubba Starling. (Seriously, he did this.) By WARP, Barnes has proven to be one of the most valuable 20-or-so relievers in the game over the past two seasons—he's in the same range as Aroldis Chapman, Kenley Jansen and Héctor Neris—but that's at least in part because he throws a lot of innings. Both for their own good and for Barnes' sake, the Red Sox need to get him some help.

YEAR	TEAM	LVL	AGE	WHIP	ERA	DRA	WARP	MPH	FB%	WHF	CSP
2017	BOS	MLB	27	1.22	3.88	3.30	1.5	97.1	55	13.2	42.7
2018	BOS	MLB	28	1.26	3.65	2.21	1.9	98.7	54.8	15	42.7
2019	BOS	MLB	29	1.38	3.78	2.75	1.8	98.4	47.3	16	38.8
2020	BOS	MLB	30	1.35	3.66	3.76	1.0	97.4	51.3	14.9	40.9

Boston Red Sox 2020

Matt Barnes, continued

Pitch Shape vs LHH

Pitch Shape vs RHH

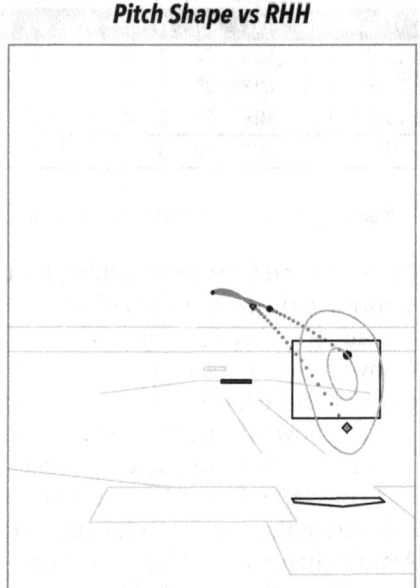

Type	Frequency	Velocity	H Movement	V Movement
● Fastball	47.3%	97 [113]	-9.2 [90]	-11 [113]
☐ Sinker				
+ Cutter				
▲ Changeup				
✕ Splitter				
▽ Slider				
◇ Curveball	50.7%	85.8 [124]	3.3 [83]	-44.3 [107]
✥ Slow Curveball				
✱ Knuckleball				
▼ Screwball				

Ryan Brasier RHP

Born: 08/26/87   Age: 32   Bats: R   Throws: R
Height: 6'0"   Weight: 225   Origin: Round 6, 2007 Draft (#208 overall)

YEAR	TEAM	LVL	AGE	W	L	SV	G	GS	IP	H	HR	BB/9	K/9	K	GB%	BABIP
2018	PAW	AAA	30	2	5	13	34	0	40^1	29	1	1.8	8.9	40	43%	.277
2018	BOS	MLB	30	2	0	0	34	0	33^2	19	2	1.9	7.8	29	43%	.198
2019	PAW	AAA	31	2	0	0	10	0	9^1	6	1	1.0	12.5	13	45%	.263
2019	BOS	MLB	31	2	4	7	62	0	55^2	51	9	3.4	9.9	61	33%	.286
2020	BOS	MLB	32	2	2	0	45	0	47	42	7	3.1	9.9	52	37%	.288

Comparables: Miguel Socolovich, Kevin Quackenbush, Justin Miller

Brasier's fall from grace was fairly dramatic even by 2019's lofty standards among hard-ass righties. The big Texan became a cult hero during the 2018 World Series run when he barked at Gary Sánchez to "get his ass back in the box," and he entered 2019 as one of the front-runners to earn saves for the Craig Kimbrel-less Red Sox. Instead, Brasier was back in Pawtucket by July. That'll happen when your walk, homer and contact allowed rates all skyrocket. Brasier was always a long shot to repeat his breakout season, but it's hard to pinpoint exactly why he regressed so quickly; while his command wavered, he still featured plus velocity and his pitch mix didn't change much. The optimists may say that points toward a potential rebound, but realists are more likely to acknowledge Brasier's 2018 as the fun fluke it was.

YEAR	TEAM	LVL	AGE	WHIP	ERA	DRA	WARP	MPH	FB%	WHF	CSP
2018	PAW	AAA	30	0.92	1.34	3.13	0.9				
2018	BOS	MLB	30	0.77	1.60	3.57	0.5	98.4	62.6	17.3	45.8
2019	PAW	AAA	31	0.75	0.96	2.26	0.4				
2019	BOS	MLB	31	1.29	4.85	5.38	0.0	97.7	59.3	16.5	44.2
2020	BOS	MLB	32	1.23	3.79	4.04	0.6	96.9	59.7	16.6	44.5

Boston Red Sox 2020

Ryan Brasier, continued

Pitch Shape vs LHH

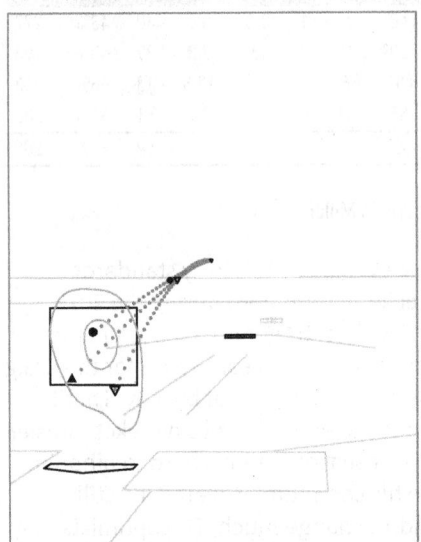

Pitch Shape vs RHH

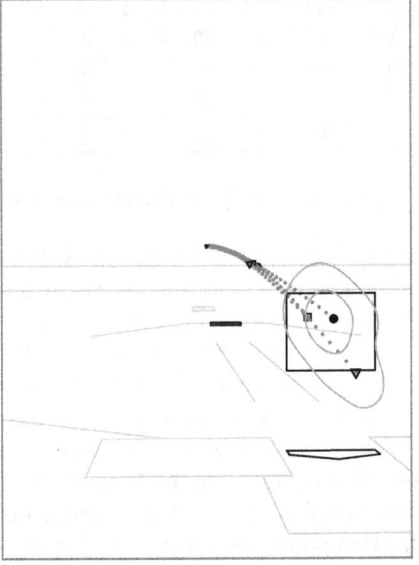

Type	Frequency	Velocity	H Movement	V Movement
● Fastball	55.5%	96.4 [112]	-5.3 [107]	-11.7 [111]
☐ Sinker	3.8%	96.4 [120]	-12.3 [102]	-15.2 [118]
+ Cutter				
▲ Changeup	8.9%	87.8 [109]	-12.1 [96]	-25.9 [104]
✕ Splitter				
▽ Slider	31.8%	85.5 [105]	6.2 [105]	-33.2 [100]
◇ Curveball				
⊕ Slow Curveball				
✶ Knuckleball				
▼ Screwball				

Colten Brewer RHP

Born: 10/29/92 Age: 27 Bats: R Throws: R
Height: 6'4" Weight: 230 Origin: Round 4, 2011 Draft (#122 overall)

YEAR	TEAM	LVL	AGE	W	L	SV	G	GS	IP	H	HR	BB/9	K/9	K	GB%	BABIP
2017	TAM	A+	24	0	0	2	6	0	9^1	3	0	1.0	14.5	15	78%	.167
2017	TRN	AA	24	3	1	11	29	0	41^1	37	0	2.4	9.4	43	64%	.314
2017	SWB	AAA	24	0	0	1	6	0	10	17	2	3.6	9.9	11	60%	.417
2018	ELP	AAA	25	3	4	3	37	0	48	40	3	2.8	11.8	63	56%	.330
2018	SDN	MLB	25	1	0	0	11	0	9^2	15	0	6.5	9.3	10	50%	.469
2019	PAW	AAA	26	2	3	0	9	0	11	14	2	5.7	8.2	10	57%	.343
2019	BOS	MLB	26	1	2	0	58	0	54^2	59	6	5.6	8.6	52	53%	.333
2020	BOS	MLB	27	2	2	0	39	0	41	41	5	4.5	8.7	40	53%	.308

Comparables: Dovydas Neverauskas, Marcus Hatley, Yacksel Ríos

Tree House. Nightshift. Trillium. Aeronaut. Lord Hobo. Notch. And yes, even Harpoon. There are no shortage of outstanding purveyors of craft beer in Greater Boston, but in Colten, the area finally hosted a Brewer that fell flat. While Brewer missed his fair share of bats, he also walked too many batters and gave up too many home runs, which helps to explain why DRA tells us his ERA overstates his effectiveness by more than a full run. Most teams don't run five or six elite relievers deep, but it says plenty about the 2019 Red Sox bullpen that Brewer was its fifth-most used option. Odds are Boston will look to have better options on tap, which means Brewer may find himself back with the Narragansetts of the world in Rhode Island.

YEAR	TEAM	LVL	AGE	WHIP	ERA	DRA	WARP	MPH	FB%	WHF	CSP
2017	TAM	A+	24	0.43	0.00	1.57	0.4				
2017	TRN	AA	24	1.16	1.31	3.39	0.7				
2017	SWB	AAA	24	2.10	11.70	7.16	-0.2				
2018	ELP	AAA	25	1.15	3.75	2.56	1.4				
2018	SDN	MLB	25	2.28	5.59	2.71	0.2	95.7	68.6	10.8	48.6
2019	PAW	AAA	26	1.91	4.91	6.54	0.0				
2019	BOS	MLB	26	1.70	4.12	5.20	0.1	95.8	44	11.7	43.7
2020	BOS	MLB	27	1.48	4.65	4.64	0.2	95.3	47.8	11.7	46.5

Boston Red Sox 2020

Colten Brewer, continued

Pitch Shape vs LHH

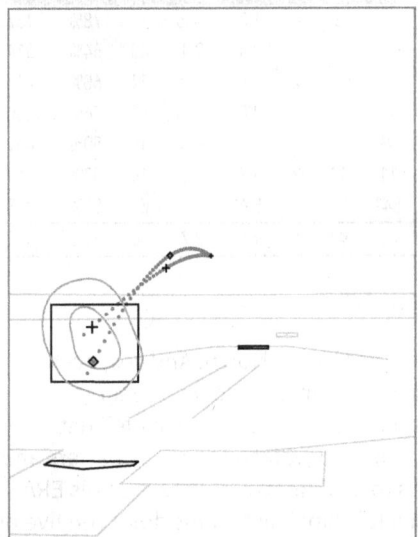

Pitch Shape vs RHH

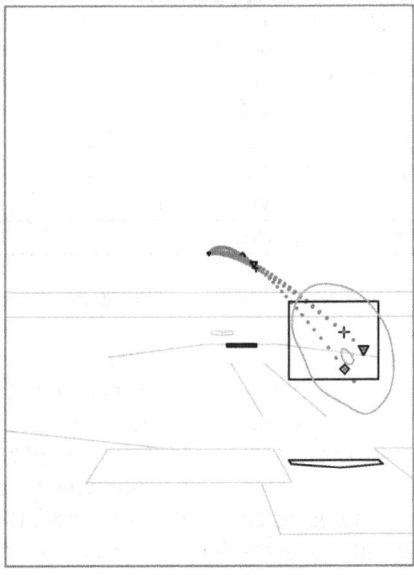

Type	Frequency	Velocity	H Movement	V Movement
● Fastball				
☐ Sinker				
+ Cutter	42.1%	93.6 [131]	2.7 [105]	-21.6 [109]
▲ Changeup				
✕ Splitter				
▽ Slider	11.4%	88.3 [117]	6.5 [106]	-30.9 [106]
◇ Curveball	44.4%	82.2 [112]	10.2 [111]	-50.9 [93]
✦ Slow Curveball				
✻ Knuckleball				
▼ Screwball				

Austin Brice RHP

Born: 06/19/92   Age: 28   Bats: R   Throws: R
Height: 6'4"   Weight: 235   Origin: Round 9, 2010 Draft (#287 overall)

YEAR	TEAM	LVL	AGE	W	L	SV	G	GS	IP	H	HR	BB/9	K/9	K	GB%	BABIP
2017	LOU	AAA	25	1	2	1	15	0	21^1	23	0	3.8	8.9	21	46%	.365
2017	CIN	MLB	25	0	0	0	22	0	32^2	33	6	1.9	7.2	26	50%	.284
2018	LOU	AAA	26	3	1	1	17	0	23^1	18	2	2.7	9.3	24	36%	.296
2018	CIN	MLB	26	2	3	0	33	0	37^1	39	9	3.1	7.7	32	53%	.286
2019	MIA	MLB	27	1	0	0	36	0	44^2	37	7	3.6	9.3	46	42%	.248
2020	*MIA*	*MLB*	*28*	*1*	*1*	*0*	*11*	*0*	*12*	*12*	*2*	*3.2*	*8.8*	*11*	*43%*	*.296*

Comparables: Jake Barrett, Victor Alcántara, Parker Bridwell

In 2019, Brice partially exorcised the home run demon that has haunted him throughout his young major league career. Considering the bizarre ball aerodynamics, that's cause for minor celebration. His four-seam fastball velocity dipped below 95 mph, but it remains a weapon against righties because of its heavy sink and he hides the ball well behind his very low three-quarters delivery. While he set a career high for innings in 2019, he still hit the IL multiple times with right forearm issues and even his attractive top-line stats weren't enough for him to be used in high-leverage situations. The all-time leader in strikeouts among pitchers born in Hong Kong has solidified a bullpen spot for now—quite possibly as a result of the all-time leader in strikeouts from Taiwan, Wei-Yin Chen, getting DFA'd.

YEAR	TEAM	LVL	AGE	WHIP	ERA	DRA	WARP	MPH	FB%	WHF	CSP
2017	LOU	AAA	25	1.50	3.80	5.20	0.0				
2017	CIN	MLB	25	1.22	4.96	4.76	0.2	96.1	62.4	11.9	51.1
2018	LOU	AAA	26	1.07	2.31	3.88	0.3				
2018	CIN	MLB	26	1.39	5.79	5.75	-0.4	96.0	68.4	10	50.1
2019	MIA	MLB	27	1.23	3.43	4.51	0.4	94.9	51	12.5	48.1
2020	*MIA*	*MLB*	*28*	*1.36*	*4.79*	*5.01*	*0.1*	*94.9*	*58.9*	*11.7*	*49.8*

Austin Brice, continued

Pitch Shape vs LHH   Pitch Shape vs RHH

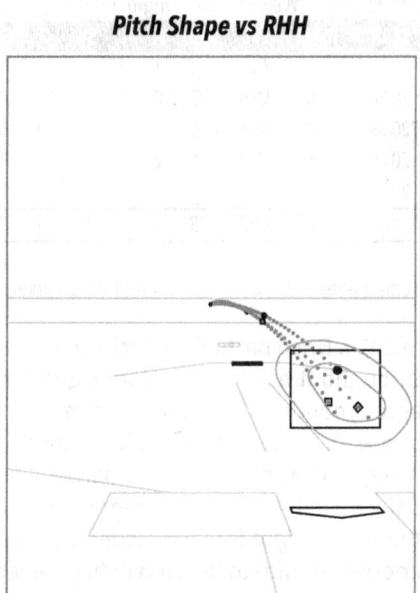

Andrew Cashner   RHP

Born: 09/11/86   Age: 33   Bats: R   Throws: R
Height: 6'6"   Weight: 235   Origin: Round 1, 2008 Draft (#19 overall)

YEAR	TEAM	LVL	AGE	W	L	SV	G	GS	IP	H	HR	BB/9	K/9	K	GB%	BABIP
2017	TEX	MLB	30	11	11	0	28	28	166^2	156	15	3.5	4.6	86	49%	.266
2018	BAL	MLB	31	4	15	0	28	28	153	177	25	3.8	5.8	99	42%	.311
2019	BAL	MLB	32	9	3	0	17	17	96^1	86	11	2.7	6.2	66	50%	.256
2019	BOS	MLB	32	2	5	1	25	6	53^2	58	8	4.9	7.0	42	49%	.325
2020	BOS	MLB	33	2	2	0	33	0	35	38	5	3.6	6.6	26	47%	.299

Comparables: Tyson Ross, Daniel Hudson, Dillon Gee

Perhaps nothing better encapsulates the difficulties the 2019 Red Sox faced on the mound than their need to trade for Cashner in mid-July. To be fair, Cashner was in the midst of his best season since 2015, what with his ERA south of 4.00 and his one WARP. His supposed evolution was attributed to a newfound ability to limit walks, and a changing pitch mix that saw Cashner favor his changeup over his sinker. But this is (Chris Traeger voice) *literally* Andrew Cashner we're talking about. It can't be that surprising that he bombed in six starts with Boston before facing relegation to the bullpen. A look at his first half in Baltimore and there is hope that league-average production can be squeezed out of him for a bit, but that's a best-case scenario at this point.

YEAR	TEAM	LVL	AGE	WHIP	ERA	DRA	WARP	MPH	FB%	WHF	CSP
2017	TEX	MLB	30	1.32	3.40	5.58	0.0	96.3	65.1	6.7	49.6
2018	BAL	MLB	31	1.58	5.29	6.69	-2.4	95.5	60.2	7.5	46.7
2019	BAL	MLB	32	1.19	3.83	4.74	1.0	96.2	50.4	9.3	47.1
2019	BOS	MLB	32	1.62	6.20	5.71	0.0	96.9	50.4	11.8	44.1
2020	BOS	MLB	33	1.48	5.03	5.05	0.1	95.0	56.8	8.3	46.5

Andrew Cashner, continued

Pitch Shape vs LHH

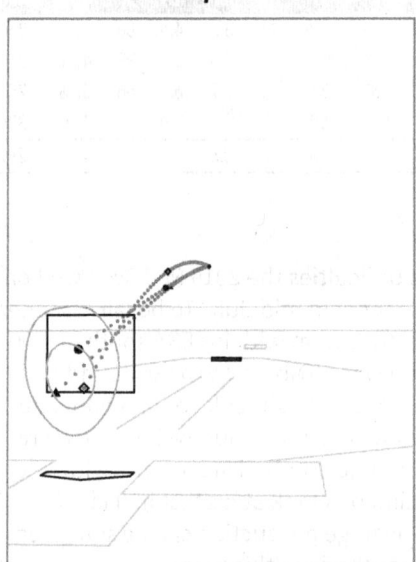

Pitch Shape vs RHH

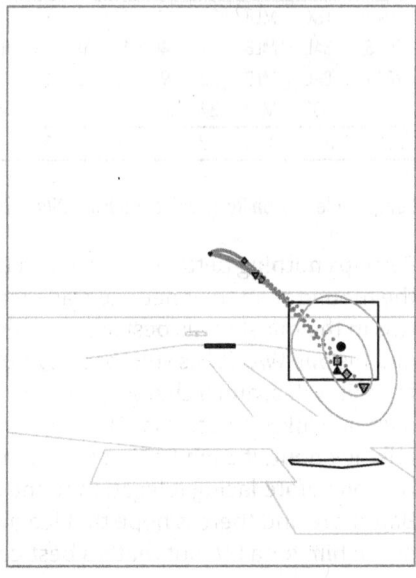

Nathan Eovaldi RHP

Born: 02/13/90   Age: 30   Bats: R   Throws: R
Height: 6'2"   Weight: 225   Origin: Round 11, 2008 Draft (#337 overall)

YEAR	TEAM	LVL	AGE	W	L	SV	G	GS	IP	H	HR	BB/9	K/9	K	GB%	BABIP
2018	PCH	A+	28	0	0	0	3	3	6	6	2	0.0	10.5	7	47%	.267
2018	TBA	MLB	28	3	4	0	10	10	57	48	11	1.3	8.4	53	48%	.245
2018	BOS	MLB	28	3	3	0	12	11	54	57	3	2.0	8.0	48	46%	.325
2019	BOS	MLB	29	2	1	0	23	12	67^2	72	16	4.7	9.3	70	45%	.315
2020	BOS	MLB	30	9	7	0	24	24	134	136	19	3.4	9.0	133	46%	.314

Comparables: Trevor Cahill, Jair Jurrjens, Randall Delgado

It's entirely possible that Eovaldi is the man who got Dave Dombrowski fired. If you squint, you can sort of see why Dombo backed up the Brinks truck for Eovaldi. The flame-throwing righty was just off his best season, came up huge for the Red Sox in October and was likely seen as Rick Porcello's replacement for 2020 and beyond. Still, there's no way to sugarcoat the fact that Dombrowski chose to give nearly $70 million to a dude with as many Tommy John surgeries as 2-WARP seasons. Sure enough, Eovaldi missed a ton of time in 2019 after undergoing a procedure to remove loose bodies from his elbow. When on the mound, he displayed all the command and accuracy of a Bob Nightengale tweet, embarrassing himself in a very short stint as Boston's closer. For a Red Sox team that's suddenly crying poor, Eovaldi's albatross of a contract is an utter disaster; one new head honcho Chaim Bloom may either try to get out from under or, at the very least, avoid replicating.

YEAR	TEAM	LVL	AGE	WHIP	ERA	DRA	WARP	MPH	FB%	WHF	CSP
2018	PCH	A+	28	1.00	4.50	3.80	0.1				
2018	TBA	MLB	28	0.98	4.26	3.19	1.4	99.0	38.2	12.7	54.7
2018	BOS	MLB	28	1.28	3.33	3.28	1.3	99.4	38.2	10.9	51.7
2019	BOS	MLB	29	1.58	5.99	6.37	-0.5	99.7	43.3	11.8	46.8
2020	BOS	MLB	30	1.40	4.54	4.62	1.4	98.6	40.5	11.8	49.5

Nathan Eovaldi, continued

Pitch Shape vs LHH	Pitch Shape vs RHH
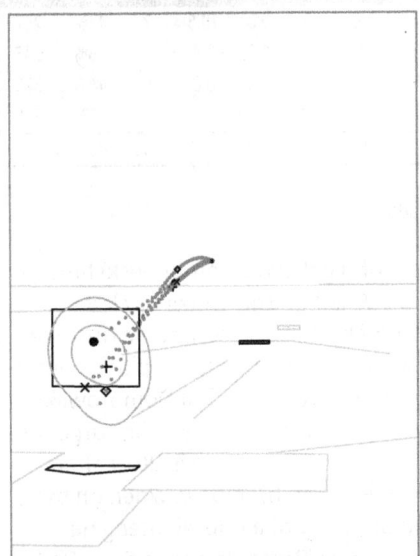	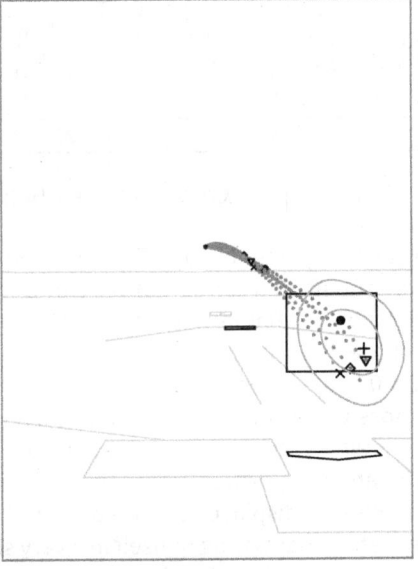

Type	Frequency	Velocity	H Movement	V Movement
● Fastball	43.3%	97.7 [115]	-9.7 [87]	-13 [108]
□ Sinker				
+ Cutter	22.5%	93.6 [131]	1 [95]	-19.5 [117]
▲ Changeup				
× Splitter	13.7%	88.2 [113]	-8.4 [98]	-30 [97]
▽ Slider	3.0%	85.4 [104]	6.8 [107]	-33 [100]
◇ Curveball	17.5%	80.7 [107]	6.9 [98]	-45.2 [105]
◈ Slow Curveball				
✹ Knuckleball				
▼ Screwball				

Heath Hembree RHP

Born: 01/13/89   Age: 31   Bats: R   Throws: R
Height: 6'4"   Weight: 210   Origin: Round 5, 2010 Draft (#168 overall)

YEAR	TEAM	LVL	AGE	W	L	SV	G	GS	IP	H	HR	BB/9	K/9	K	GB%	BABIP
2017	BOS	MLB	28	2	3	0	62	0	62	72	10	2.6	10.2	70	42%	.360
2018	BOS	MLB	29	4	1	0	67	0	60	53	10	4.1	11.4	76	40%	.295
2019	BOS	MLB	30	1	0	2	45	0	39²	34	7	4.1	10.4	46	24%	.273
2020	BOS	MLB	31	2	2	0	45	0	47	40	8	3.5	9.7	51	32%	.269

Comparables: Kevin Quackenbush, Chase Whitley, Jeremy Accardo

June 14 might not have been a very memorable day for you, but for Hembree, it marked the beginning of the end. Up until that point, he owned a 2.51 ERA, had only allowed a run in six of his 31 appearances and had been especially dominant since May 1 (0.60 ERA). Unfortunately, Hembree's season was derailed by an extensor strain in his right elbow, which knocked him out until July 5. He was never the same upon his return, allowing nine earned runs in nine innings over his next 12 appearances before returning to the IL on August 2. Hembree got a PRP injection in his balky joint and reappeared at the very end of the year for two final appearances, but by then it was far too late to save either his season or Boston's. DRA tells us Hembree was getting lucky even during his hot stretch, and as such he remains nothing more than a serviceable arm who can soak up low-to-moderate leverage innings. When his arm is healthy, that is.

YEAR	TEAM	LVL	AGE	WHIP	ERA	DRA	WARP	MPH	FB%	WHF	CSP
2017	BOS	MLB	28	1.45	3.63	3.39	1.2	97.7	53.1	15.2	45.3
2018	BOS	MLB	29	1.33	4.20	3.87	0.7	96.8	54.9	15.5	45.3
2019	BOS	MLB	30	1.31	3.86	6.54	-0.5	96.0	69.9	13.3	45.5
2020	BOS	MLB	31	1.25	3.98	4.21	0.5	95.9	58.8	14.6	45.1

Boston Red Sox 2020

Heath Hembree, continued

Pitch Shape vs LHH   Pitch Shape vs RHH

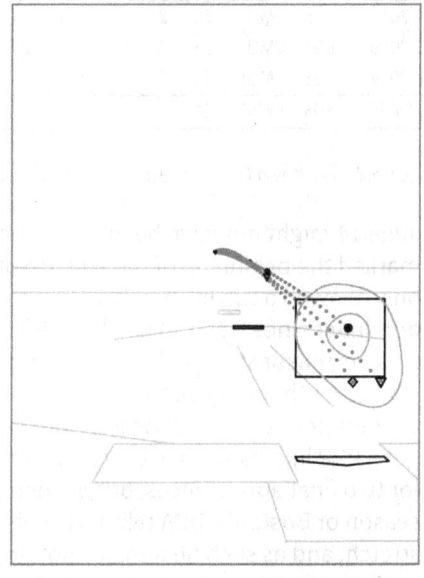

Type	Frequency	Velocity	H Movement	V Movement
● Fastball	69.8%	94 [104]	-6.5 [102]	-12.5 [109]
☐ Sinker				
+ Cutter				
▲ Changeup				
✕ Splitter				
▽ Slider	16.1%	87.8 [114]	2.5 [89]	-25.8 [121]
◇ Curveball	14.0%	82 [111]	8.9 [106]	-42.9 [110]
◈ Slow Curveball				
✴ Knuckleball				
▼ Screwball				

Darwinzon Hernandez LHP

Born: 12/17/96   Age: 23   Bats: L   Throws: L
Height: 6'2"   Weight: 245   Origin: International Free Agent, 2013

YEAR	TEAM	LVL	AGE	W	L	SV	G	GS	IP	H	HR	BB/9	K/9	K	GB%	BABIP
2017	GRN	A	20	4	5	0	23	23	103^1	85	8	4.3	10.1	116	50%	.292
2018	SLM	A+	21	9	5	0	23	23	101	80	1	5.3	11.0	124	46%	.326
2018	PME	AA	21	0	0	0	5	0	6	6	0	9.0	15.0	10	36%	.429
2019	PME	AA	22	1	4	0	10	9	40^1	33	2	7.1	13.2	59	39%	.337
2019	PAW	AAA	22	1	2	0	7	3	17	10	2	8.5	10.6	20	38%	.229
2019	BOS	MLB	22	0	1	0	29	1	30^1	27	1	7.7	16.9	57	44%	.433
2020	BOS	MLB	23	3	3	0	38	5	55	40	7	5.1	12.5	76	39%	.280

Comparables: Touki Toussaint, Enny Romero, Mitch Atkins

Thirty innings is often too small a sample size from which to derive anything meaningful, but in his first 30 frames in the big leagues, Hernandez told us *exactly* who he was. No one with as many innings pitched—not Josh Hader, nor Edwin Díaz nor Nick Anderson—struck out more batters per inning. At the same time, only one pitcher with as many innings—José Alvarado—issued walks at a higher rate. That's Hernandez to a tee; a chonky, flamethrowing lefty who can strike out any hitter on the planet, but who could also find a way to give a windmill first base. There's a chance this is as good as it'll ever get for Hernandez, but if he can improve his command even just a little, we might be looking at the new poster child for Effectively Wild. Fortunately, his first name suggests he should be open to evolving.

YEAR	TEAM	LVL	AGE	WHIP	ERA	DRA	WARP	MPH	FB%	WHF	CSP
2017	GRN	A	20	1.30	4.01	4.11	1.4				
2018	SLM	A+	21	1.39	3.56	4.15	1.4				
2018	PME	AA	21	2.00	3.00	4.27	0.0				
2019	PME	AA	22	1.61	5.13	5.03	-0.1				
2019	PAW	AAA	22	1.53	4.76	4.70	0.3				
2019	BOS	MLB	22	1.75	4.45	3.04	0.8	97.7	74.2	14.7	47.3
2020	BOS	MLB	23	1.29	3.58	3.70	1.0	97.6	76.9	15.2	49

Boston Red Sox 2020

Darwinzon Hernandez, continued

Pitch Shape vs LHH

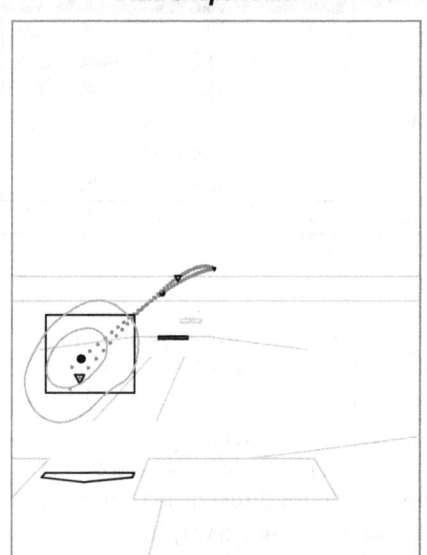

Pitch Shape vs RHH

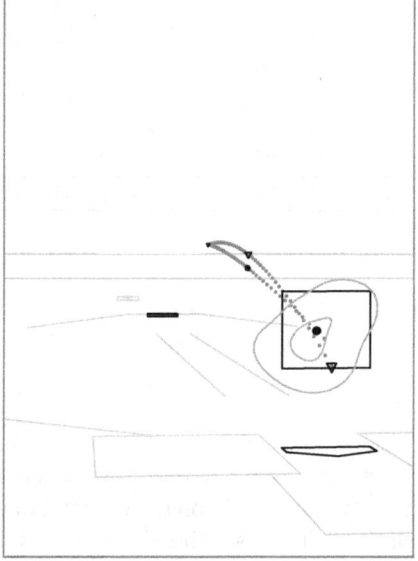

Type	Frequency	Velocity	H Movement	V Movement
● Fastball	74.2%	95.6 [109]	2.6 [119]	-15 [103]
☐ Sinker				
+ Cutter				
▲ Changeup				
✕ Splitter				
▽ Slider	24.9%	82.9 [94]	-7.5 [110]	-39.1 [83]
◇ Curveball				
⬥ Slow Curveball				
✴ Knuckleball				
▼ Screwball				

Josh Osich LHP

Born: 09/03/88 Age: 31 Bats: L Throws: L
Height: 6'3" Weight: 232 Origin: Round 6, 2011 Draft (#207 overall)

YEAR	TEAM	LVL	AGE	W	L	SV	G	GS	IP	H	HR	BB/9	K/9	K	GB%	BABIP
2017	SAC	AAA	28	1	1	2	9	0	9^1	12	0	2.9	7.7	8	55%	.364
2017	SFN	MLB	28	3	2	0	54	0	43^1	48	7	5.6	8.9	43	46%	.333
2018	SAC	AAA	29	0	0	0	37	2	45^1	56	2	3.6	8.3	42	47%	.365
2018	SFN	MLB	29	0	0	0	12	0	12	20	2	5.2	7.5	10	45%	.450
2019	CHA	MLB	30	4	0	0	57	0	67^2	62	15	2.0	8.1	61	42%	.260
2020	BOS	MLB	31	1	1	0	17	0	18	17	3	3.4	9.0	18	45%	.297

Comparables: Bobby LaFromboise, Sam Freeman, Javy Guerra

For about five seconds each time Josh Osich jogged out from the bullpen during White Sox home games, fans had to wonder what was going on as the delicate opening licks of Fleetwood Mac's "The Chain" aired on the Guaranteed Rate Field speaker system. By the time the longtime Giant, oft-time Triple-A River Cat arrived in White Sox camp in the middle of March, he was on his third organization of the spring, and being allowed five seconds in the majors to set the mood didn't seem like something that was in his future. Osich certainly didn't do anything in 2019 to make any team reserve a place for him in their future plans. But for the first time in four years, the burly, hard-throwing lefty, didn't make everyone wonder what he was doing in the big leagues in the first place, either. He doesn't throw that hard anymore, but more by choice as he's flipped to a cutter-heavy approach that strangely has improved his strike-throwing. Far too many of those strikes still wound up in the seats, but it feels like an accomplishment these days when a guy gets cut by the Orioles and it's not the end of his career.

YEAR	TEAM	LVL	AGE	WHIP	ERA	DRA	WARP	MPH	FB%	WHF	CSP
2017	SAC	AAA	28	1.61	7.71	4.35	0.1				
2017	SFN	MLB	28	1.73	6.23	5.62	-0.2	97.5	54.7	10	46.7
2018	SAC	AAA	29	1.63	4.96	5.10	0.0				
2018	SFN	MLB	29	2.25	8.25	6.64	-0.2	97.4	48.5	14.1	49.6
2019	CHA	MLB	30	1.14	4.66	4.49	0.6	95.6	16.9	13.4	48.3
2020	BOS	MLB	31	1.36	4.48	4.63	0.1	95.4	30.3	12.5	48

Josh Osich, continued

Pitch Shape vs LHH

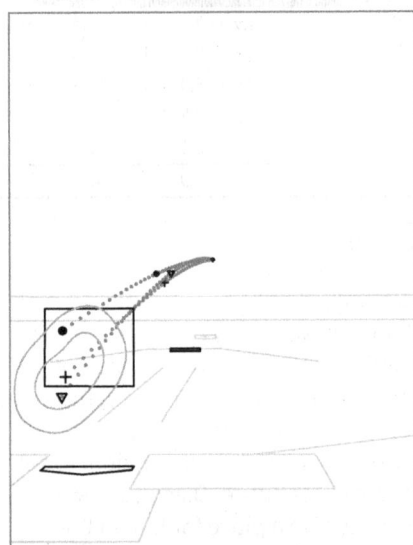

Pitch Shape vs RHH

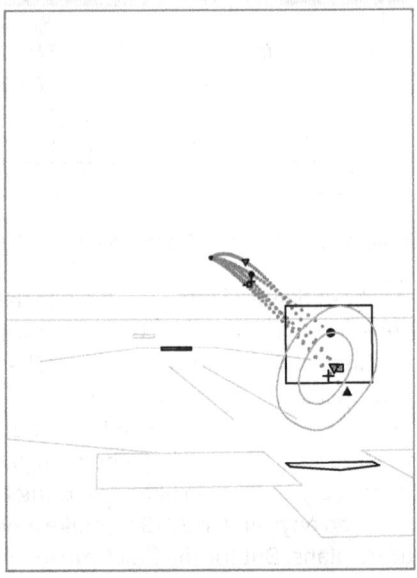

Type	Frequency	Velocity	H Movement	V Movement
● Fastball	10.3%	94.8 [107]	4.3 [112]	-16.1 [100]
□ Sinker	6.5%	94.6 [110]	13.1 [97]	-19.9 [102]
+ Cutter	65.0%	89.6 [106]	-1.7 [99]	-24.6 [98]
▲ Changeup	4.7%	84.2 [96]	11 [101]	-22.5 [114]
✕ Splitter				
▽ Slider	13.4%	79.7 [80]	-0.9 [83]	-41.6 [75]
◇ Curveball				
✦ Slow Curveball				
✳ Knuckleball				
▼ Screwball				

Martín Pérez LHP

Born: 04/04/91 Age: 29 Bats: L Throws: L
Height: 6'0" Weight: 200 Origin: International Free Agent, 2007

YEAR	TEAM	LVL	AGE	W	L	SV	G	GS	IP	H	HR	BB/9	K/9	K	GB%	BABIP
2017	TEX	MLB	26	13	12	0	32	32	185	221	23	3.1	5.6	115	48%	.328
2018	FRI	AA	27	1	0	0	1	1	6	2	0	4.5	6.0	4	65%	.118
2018	ROU	AAA	27	1	0	0	1	1	6^1	6	1	0.0	8.5	6	72%	.294
2018	TEX	MLB	27	2	7	0	22	15	85^1	116	16	3.8	5.5	52	52%	.344
2019	MIN	MLB	28	10	7	0	32	29	165^1	184	23	3.6	7.3	135	49%	.316
2020	BOS	MLB	29	7	6	0	23	23	98	108	13	3.6	7.2	78	50%	.314

Comparables: Jordan Lyles, Matt Harrison, Chris Haney

Left-handed pitchers have career paths that don't end until the last pasta bowl hits an Olive Garden table. And when one of 'em shows up in March of their age-28 season with a couple extra ticks on an already-fast fastball as well as a shiny new cutter? Well, they're upgraded to the Lifetime Pasta Pass. Pérez is going to need all the carbs he can get to land future opportunities. The seemingly turbo-charged four-seamer was bashed by hitters, who slugged .729 against it. Predictably, he posted his fifth consecutive negative-WARP season; an impressive run of mediocrity, to be sure, but one that's not going to cut it for a team with 100-win aspirations. Pérez signed a one-year deal with Boston, where he'll try to avoid the clam chowder bowl.

YEAR	TEAM	LVL	AGE	WHIP	ERA	DRA	WARP	MPH	FB%	WHF	CSP
2017	TEX	MLB	26	1.54	4.82	7.09	-3.1	95.4	58.7	8	41.1
2018	FRI	AA	27	0.83	0.00	3.02	0.2				
2018	ROU	AAA	27	0.95	1.42	3.41	0.2				
2018	TEX	MLB	27	1.78	6.22	7.31	-2.0	95.5	67.3	8.2	48.8
2019	MIN	MLB	28	1.52	5.12	6.32	-1.0	96.2	42.3	10.5	46.1
2020	BOS	MLB	29	1.50	4.89	4.89	0.8	95.1	52.5	9.2	45.8

Boston Red Sox 2020

Martín Pérez, continued

Pitch Shape vs LHH

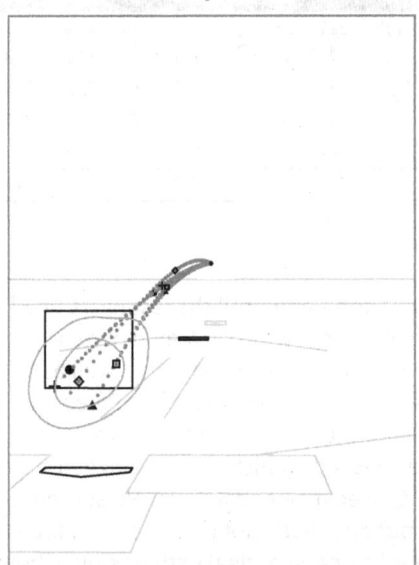

Pitch Shape vs RHH

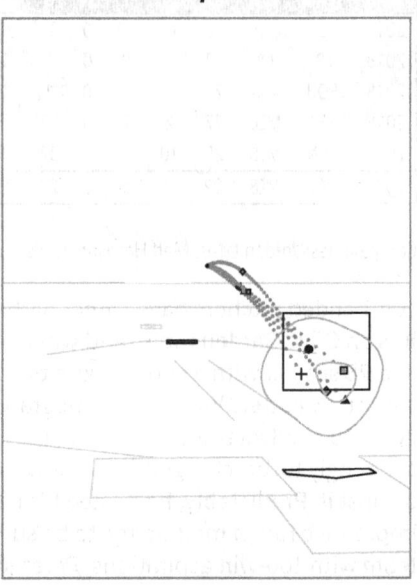

Type	Frequency	Velocity	H Movement	V Movement
● Fastball	16.9%	94.5 [106]	8.7 [92]	-13.8 [106]
☐ Sinker	25.4%	94.2 [108]	15 [85]	-19 [105]
+ Cutter	30.9%	88.8 [101]	-2.1 [101]	-24.8 [97]
▲ Changeup	22.1%	85.6 [101]	13.5 [89]	-24.7 [108]
✕ Splitter				
▽ Slider				
◇ Curveball	4.7%	79.5 [103]	-4.2 [87]	-44.3 [107]
✦ Slow Curveball				
✳ Knuckleball				
▼ Screwball				

Eduardo Rodriguez   LHP
Born: 04/07/93   Age: 27   Bats: L   Throws: L
Height: 6'2"   Weight: 220   Origin: International Free Agent, 2010

YEAR	TEAM	LVL	AGE	W	L	SV	G	GS	IP	H	HR	BB/9	K/9	K	GB%	BABIP
2017	PAW	AAA	24	0	1	0	2	2	10^1	10	0	4.4	10.5	12	38%	.385
2017	BOS	MLB	24	6	7	0	25	24	137^1	126	19	3.3	9.8	150	36%	.299
2018	PME	AA	25	0	0	0	2	2	8	3	0	4.5	15.8	14	69%	.231
2018	BOS	MLB	25	13	5	0	27	23	129^2	119	16	3.1	10.1	146	39%	.301
2019	BOS	MLB	26	19	6	0	34	34	203^1	195	24	3.3	9.4	213	50%	.317
2020	BOS	MLB	27	11	8	0	28	28	157	151	22	3.5	9.7	169	46%	.308

Comparables: Robbie Ray, Aaron Sanchez, Brad Hand

The 2019 Red Sox enjoyed relatively few bright spots on the mound, but Rodriguez served as a welcome exception. It's hard to find a pitching category in which Rodriguez did not post a career-best mark, from strikeout rate to ERA to WARP to ground-ball rate to innings pitched. That last stat is particularly telling, as E-Rod finally went a full season without succumbing to the leg injuries that have derailed many of his previous attempts at putting it all together. Rodriguez was a top-40 overall starting pitcher, besting more celebrated AL-East arms like Marcus Stroman, James Paxton and even Blake Snell. Given that the Sox still have Chris Sale and David Price on payroll, they must hope Rodriguez doesn't need to front their rotation. But it's awfully nice to know that, health permitting, he can if he needs to.

YEAR	TEAM	LVL	AGE	WHIP	ERA	DRA	WARP	MPH	FB%	WHF	CSP
2017	PAW	AAA	24	1.45	4.35	4.35	0.2				
2017	BOS	MLB	24	1.28	4.19	4.37	1.8	95.4	65.3	12.4	44
2018	PME	AA	25	0.88	0.00	1.74	0.3				
2018	BOS	MLB	25	1.26	3.82	3.77	2.3	95.3	51.6	12.4	46.4
2019	BOS	MLB	26	1.33	3.81	4.46	2.9	94.9	54.6	12.7	43.9
2020	BOS	MLB	27	1.35	4.18	4.32	2.2	94.6	56.7	12.7	45.3

Eduardo Rodriguez, continued

Pitch Shape vs LHH

Pitch Shape vs RHH

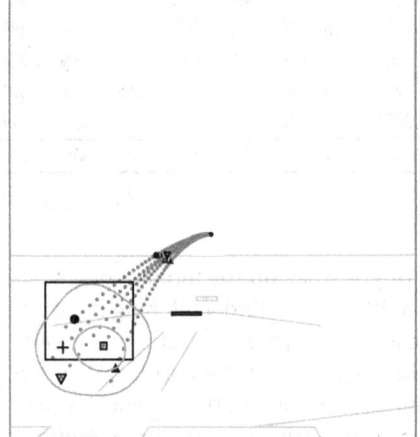
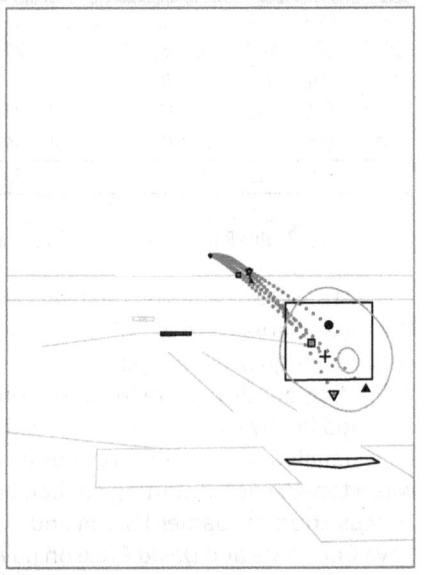

Type	Frequency	Velocity	H Movement	V Movement
● Fastball	40.3%	93.3 [102]	8 [95]	-16 [100]
☐ Sinker	14.3%	93.1 [102]	13.7 [93]	-19.4 [103]
+ Cutter	17.3%	88.8 [100]	-1.1 [95]	-23.9 [101]
▲ Changeup	23.6%	87.9 [109]	15.5 [80]	-26.8 [102]
✕ Splitter				
▽ Slider	4.5%	82.8 [93]	-3.8 [95]	-38 [86]
◇ Curveball				
⊕ Slow Curveball				
✱ Knuckleball				
▼ Screwball				

Chris Sale LHP

Born: 03/30/89   Age: 31   Bats: L   Throws: L
Height: 6'6"   Weight: 180   Origin: Round 1, 2010 Draft (#13 overall)

YEAR	TEAM	LVL	AGE	W	L	SV	G	GS	IP	H	HR	BB/9	K/9	K	GB%	BABIP
2017	BOS	MLB	28	17	8	0	32	32	214[1]	165	24	1.8	12.9	308	40%	.301
2018	BOS	MLB	29	12	4	0	27	27	158	102	11	1.9	13.5	237	45%	.283
2019	BOS	MLB	30	6	11	0	25	25	147[1]	123	24	2.3	13.3	218	44%	.309
2020	BOS	MLB	31	13	6	0	26	26	168	130	21	2.3	12.7	237	42%	.297

Comparables: Pedro Martinez, Johan Santana, Sandy Koufax

Sale is lucky that David Benioff and D.B. Weiss exist because otherwise he'd serve as 2019's most disastrous example of subverting expectations. Fresh off of signing a five-year, $145 million contract extension, Sale had his worst season since 2011. He still missed plenty of bats, and yes, he became the fastest pitcher ever to 2,000 strikeouts, but his homer and walk rates jumped while his velocity diminished. That alone would be troubling enough, but to make matters much, much worse, Sale hit the IL in mid-August with left elbow inflammation, necessitating a trip to the equally esteemed and dreaded Dr. James Andrews. The silver lining here is that Sale was *not* found to require Tommy John surgery, received a PRP injection instead, and is reportedly expected to be all systems go once spring training rolls around. People have doubted Sale's ability to stay healthy his entire career, and for the most part, they've been wrong. But he'll start this season as a 31-year-old with recent elbow and shoulder injuries who hasn't been at his best in about 18 months. If you think this has a happy ending...

YEAR	TEAM	LVL	AGE	WHIP	ERA	DRA	WARP	MPH	FB%	WHF	CSP
2017	BOS	MLB	28	0.97	2.90	2.51	7.3	97.7	50.5	15.8	48.3
2018	BOS	MLB	29	0.86	2.11	2.24	5.6	99.2	50.1	16.9	49.4
2019	BOS	MLB	30	1.09	4.40	2.93	4.5	96.9	46.3	15.1	50.2
2020	BOS	MLB	31	1.02	2.63	3.00	4.8	97.0	48.5	15.8	49.2

Boston Red Sox 2020

Chris Sale, continued

Pitch Shape vs LHH

Pitch Shape vs RHH

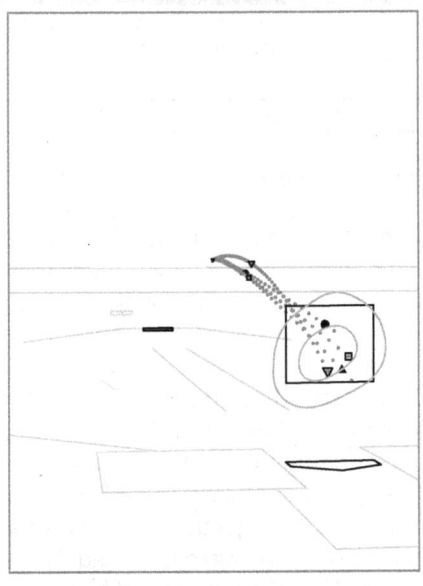

Type	Frequency	Velocity	H Movement	V Movement
● Fastball	36.0%	93.8 [104]	13.1 [72]	-17.4 [96]
☐ Sinker	10.3%	92.4 [99]	17.3 [70]	-24.9 [84]
+ Cutter				
▲ Changeup	15.3%	85.6 [101]	16.9 [73]	-34.2 [80]
✕ Splitter				
▽ Slider	38.4%	79.3 [79]	-11.9 [129]	-43.1 [71]
◇ Curveball				
⊕ Slow Curveball				
✱ Knuckleball				
▼ Screwball				

Josh Taylor LHP

Born: 03/02/93 Age: 27 Bats: L Throws: L
Height: 6'5" Weight: 225 Origin: Undrafted Free Agent, 2014

YEAR	TEAM	LVL	AGE	W	L	SV	G	GS	IP	H	HR	BB/9	K/9	K	GB%	BABIP
2017	WTN	AA	24	4	7	1	33	14	97	115	7	4.3	8.4	91	50%	.371
2018	VIS	A+	25	1	2	5	14	0	16	16	1	2.8	11.2	20	45%	.366
2018	PME	AA	25	2	5	8	33	0	35^2	42	1	4.5	9.3	37	54%	.376
2019	PAW	AAA	26	1	1	3	20	0	23^1	18	2	4.2	12.3	32	53%	.314
2019	BOS	MLB	26	2	2	0	52	1	47^1	40	5	3.0	11.8	62	46%	.321
2020	BOS	MLB	27	2	2	0	45	0	47	40	6	4.0	12.0	63	47%	.307

Comparables: Sandy Baez, Jake Jewell, Reed Garrett

Sure, it may not be the trade for a southpaw that Dave Dombrowski is best remembered by, but acquiring Taylor for Deven Marrero back in 2018 is starting to look like a pretty shrewd move. Taylor finally improved his command enough to let his plus fastball/slider combo play up in the majors and initial results were quite promising. Taylor held lefties to a .203/.247/.304 line, proving to be a devastating weapon against same-side hitters. But he also held his own against righties and in high-leverage situations en route to finishing fifth among Red Sox relievers in DRA. Taylor will already be 27 when next season starts and his upside is capped by his touch-and-go control, but barring a massive influx of talent, he's earned a spot in Boston's bullpen.

YEAR	TEAM	LVL	AGE	WHIP	ERA	DRA	WARP	MPH	FB%	WHF	CSP
2017	WTN	AA	24	1.66	5.01	7.15	-2.4				
2018	VIS	A+	25	1.31	2.81	4.36	0.1				
2018	PME	AA	25	1.68	3.79	6.09	-0.5				
2019	PAW	AAA	26	1.24	2.70	2.94	0.7				
2019	BOS	MLB	26	1.18	3.04	3.94	0.7	96.5	60.4	16.2	42.3
2020	BOS	MLB	27	1.28	3.62	3.79	0.7	96.0	61.1	16.4	42.8

Boston Red Sox 2020

Josh Taylor, continued

Pitch Shape vs LHH

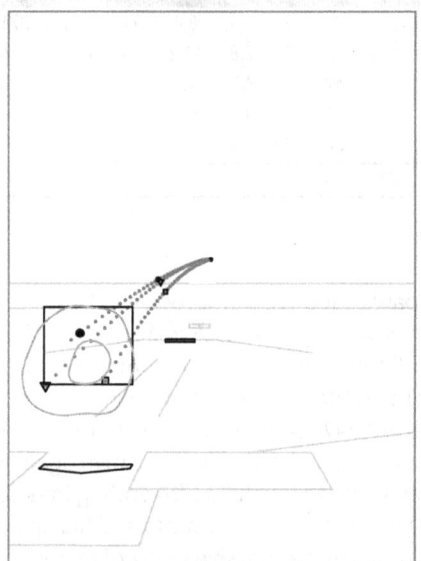

Pitch Shape vs RHH

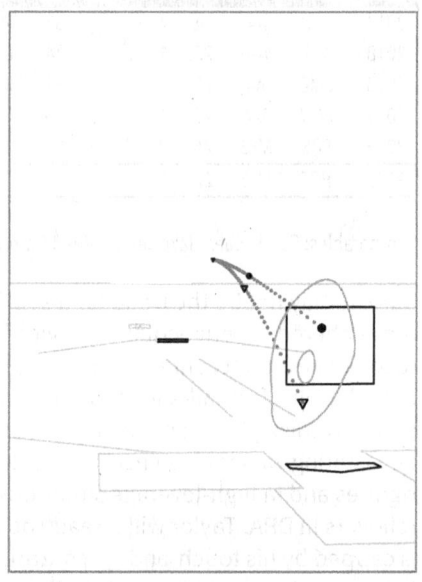

Type	Frequency	Velocity	H Movement	V Movement
● Fastball	46.8%	95 [108]	4.6 [110]	-12.5 [109]
☐ Sinker	13.6%	95 [112]	12.4 [101]	-16.8 [113]
＋ Cutter				
▲ Changeup				
✕ Splitter				
▽ Slider	37.8%	87.6 [114]	-3.5 [94]	-28 [115]
◇ Curveball				
✤ Slow Curveball				
✳ Knuckleball				
▼ Screwball				

Hector Velázquez RHP

Born: 11/26/88 Age: 31 Bats: R Throws: R
Height: 6'0" Weight: 180 Origin: International Free Agent, 2017

YEAR	TEAM	LVL	AGE	W	L	SV	G	GS	IP	H	HR	BB/9	K/9	K	GB%	BABIP
2017	PAW	AAA	28	8	4	0	19	19	102	78	7	2.1	7.0	79	45%	.251
2017	BOS	MLB	28	3	1	0	8	3	24²	21	4	2.6	6.9	19	44%	.258
2018	BOS	MLB	29	7	2	0	47	8	85	97	7	2.8	5.6	53	50%	.325
2019	PAW	AAA	30	0	0	1	12	0	16¹	11	3	6.1	7.7	14	46%	.211
2019	BOS	MLB	30	1	4	0	34	8	56¹	58	7	4.5	7.8	49	37%	.319
2020	BOS	MLB	31	3	3	0	34	6	55	58	8	3.6	7.1	44	44%	.297

Comparables: Josh Tomlin, Vinnie Chulk, Jose Cabrera

Velázquez's best ability is availability, and in 2019 he was too often unable to deliver. Back-to-back back strains strained Velázquez's ability to serve as Boston's primary swingman, leading to a marked decrease in innings and appearances. But it wasn't just Velázquez's durability that faltered; his performance did, too. Career-worst marks in DRA, homer rate and walk rate led to Velázquez performing in the bottom 50 among all pitchers who threw at least 50 innings. He's cheap enough that the Red Sox could decide to keep him around for another go, but when your ceiling is "well, he's available," you're always in the DFA danger zone.

YEAR	TEAM	LVL	AGE	WHIP	ERA	DRA	WARP	MPH	FB%	WHF	CSP
2017	PAW	AAA	28	1.00	2.21	2.95	3.1				
2017	BOS	MLB	28	1.14	2.92	4.88	0.1	92.2	68.9	8.6	51.2
2018	BOS	MLB	29	1.45	3.18	5.61	-0.5	93.6	59.2	9	46.7
2019	PAW	AAA	30	1.35	3.31	4.99	0.2				
2019	BOS	MLB	30	1.53	5.43	6.56	-0.6	94.0	50.7	10.8	44.8
2020	BOS	MLB	31	1.45	4.88	4.93	0.3	92.8	56.2	9.6	46.8

Hector Velázquez, continued

Pitch Shape vs LHH

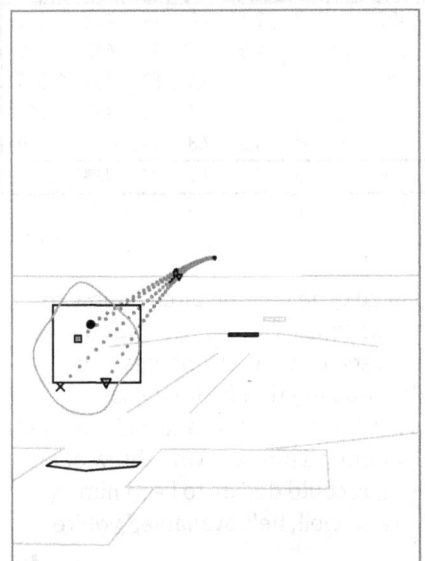

Pitch Shape vs RHH

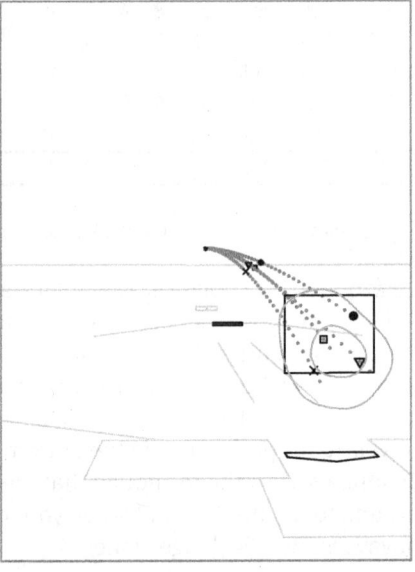

Type	Frequency	Velocity	H Movement	V Movement
● Fastball	23.6%	92.6 [101]	-6.8 [100]	-14.4 [104]
□ Sinker	27.0%	91.5 [94]	-12.9 [98]	-19.5 [103]
+ Cutter				
▲ Changeup				
✕ Splitter	30.5%	86.3 [105]	-8.1 [99]	-27.5 [106]
▽ Slider	16.5%	83.4 [96]	6.3 [105]	-29.6 [110]
◇ Curveball				
⬥ Slow Curveball				
✱ Knuckleball				
▼ Screwball				

Marcus Walden RHP

Born: 09/13/88   Age: 31   Bats: R   Throws: R
Height: 6'0"   Weight: 195   Origin: Round 9, 2007 Draft (#295 overall)

YEAR	TEAM	LVL	AGE	W	L	SV	G	GS	IP	H	HR	BB/9	K/9	K	GB%	BABIP
2017	PAW	AAA	28	10	6	0	29	15	105^2	102	4	3.1	7.3	86	54%	.312
2018	PAW	AAA	29	0	4	2	18	5	32^2	44	2	4.7	6.6	24	53%	.365
2018	BOS	MLB	29	0	0	1	8	0	14^2	14	0	1.8	8.6	14	58%	.341
2019	BOS	MLB	30	9	2	2	70	0	78	61	6	3.7	8.8	76	56%	.264
2020	BOS	MLB	31	3	3	0	61	0	65	60	8	4.0	9.4	68	54%	.300

Comparables: Murphy Smith, Drew Gagnon, Steven Wright

The Red Sox faced plenty of warranted criticism for deciding to replace Craig Kimbrel and Joe Kelly with a collection of largely anonymous dudes, but don't blame Walden for any shortcomings in that strategy. Only 12 pitchers in the big leagues threw more innings in relief, and of that dozen, only three—Liam Hendriks, Michael Lorenzen and Seth Lugo—had lower DRAs. Walden was also the fourth-best Red Sox reliever, as well as their third-most valuable fireman by WARP. He doesn't have closer stuff and isn't suited to serve in the type of super-reliever role that's currently en vogue, but Walden can eat some medium-leverage innings at an above league-average rate while making a below-market salary. For a team facing (self-imposed) payroll limitations, that's a bigger deal than it may seem.

YEAR	TEAM	LVL	AGE	WHIP	ERA	DRA	WARP	MPH	FB%	WHF	CSP
2017	PAW	AAA	28	1.31	3.92	4.04	1.8				
2018	PAW	AAA	29	1.87	4.96	6.66	-0.5				
2018	BOS	MLB	29	1.16	3.68	3.18	0.3	96.1	45.1	12.7	49
2019	BOS	MLB	30	1.19	3.81	3.83	1.3	95.8	34.7	14.1	42.9
2020	BOS	MLB	31	1.37	4.21	4.30	0.6	95.0	35.7	13.9	45.3

Boston Red Sox 2020

Marcus Walden, continued

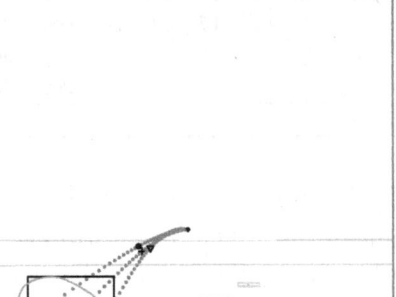

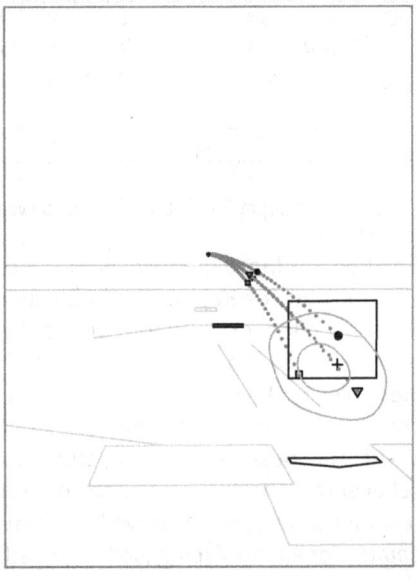

Type	Frequency	Velocity	H Movement	V Movement
● Fastball	18.0%	94.6 [106]	-2.7 [118]	-17.4 [96]
□ Sinker	16.7%	94.4 [109]	-10 [117]	-22.2 [93]
+ Cutter	28.2%	92.1 [122]	2.1 [101]	-23.1 [104]
▲ Changeup				
✕ Splitter				
▽ Slider	37.1%	85.9 [106]	9.5 [119]	-34.7 [95]
◇ Curveball				
✦ Slow Curveball				
✱ Knuckleball				
▼ Screwball				

Brandon Workman   RHP

Born: 08/13/88   Age: 31   Bats: R   Throws: R
Height: 6'5"   Weight: 235   Origin: Round 2, 2010 Draft (#57 overall)

YEAR	TEAM	LVL	AGE	W	L	SV	G	GS	IP	H	HR	BB/9	K/9	K	GB%	BABIP
2017	PAW	AAA	28	4	1	2	18	0	29	16	1	4.0	10.9	35	46%	.234
2017	BOS	MLB	28	1	1	0	33	0	39^2	37	7	2.5	8.4	37	44%	.283
2018	PAW	AAA	29	2	1	1	17	0	30	21	3	1.5	10.2	34	40%	.247
2018	BOS	MLB	29	6	1	0	43	0	41^1	34	6	3.5	8.1	37	46%	.259
2019	BOS	MLB	30	10	1	16	73	0	71^2	29	1	5.7	13.1	104	53%	.209
2020	*BOS*	*MLB*	*31*	*3*	*3*	*34*	*61*	*0*	*65*	*54*	*8*	*4.4*	*11.5*	*83*	*49%*	*.300*

Comparables: Justin Grimm, Tyler Duffey, A.J. Griffin

Why choose between being lucky or good when you can be both? Workman was Boston's best reliever in 2019. An uptick in velocity and increased reliance on his nasty curveball led to a drastic increase in strikeouts; he earned whiffs at a rate commensurate with big-name relievers like Will Smith, Brad Hand and José Leclerc. Workman was durable, performed well in high-leverage situations and ended up leading the Sox in saves. It was quite the redemption story for a dude who got bumped from the 2018 World Series roster in favor of Drew Pomeranz, but it's fair to question how sustainable Workman's performance will prove to be. Among pitchers who threw at least 50 innings, he had the eighth-highest walk rate. He led all of baseball in suppressing homers, despite allowing them at an above average rate throughout his career. And he held opposing batters to a BABIP near the Mendoza Line. DRA tells us this wasn't all luck and that Workman can be a solid reliever moving forward. But if the Sox enter 2020 with him poised to serve as their best bullpen option, they'll be asking for trouble.

YEAR	TEAM	LVL	AGE	WHIP	ERA	DRA	WARP	MPH	FB%	WHF	CSP
2017	PAW	AAA	28	1.00	1.55	2.48	0.9				
2017	BOS	MLB	28	1.21	3.18	3.68	0.7	94.9	51.4	11.3	45.9
2018	PAW	AAA	29	0.87	3.90	2.93	0.8				
2018	BOS	MLB	29	1.21	3.27	6.21	-0.6	93.3	38.9	11.1	48.1
2019	BOS	MLB	30	1.03	1.88	2.86	1.9	94.8	33.6	13.6	41.2
2020	*BOS*	*MLB*	*31*	*1.32*	*3.63*	*3.78*	*1.0*	*93.6*	*37.7*	*12.5*	*44.4*

Boston Red Sox 2020

Brandon Workman, continued

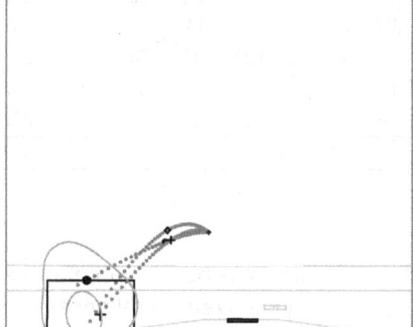
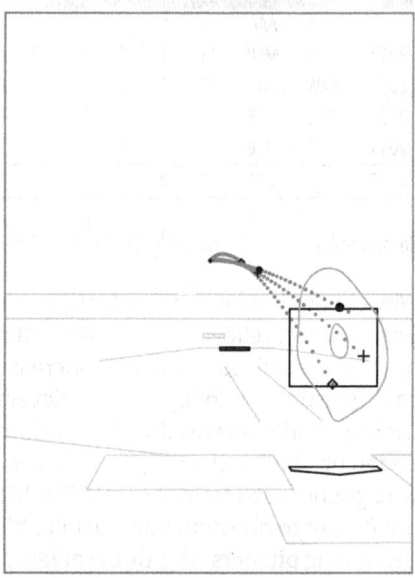

Type	Frequency	Velocity	H Movement	V Movement
● Fastball	33.6%	93.3 [103]	-2.2 [121]	-12.5 [109]
□ Sinker				
+ Cutter	19.0%	87.4 [92]	4.1 [113]	-29 [82]
▲ Changeup				
✕ Splitter				
▽ Slider				
◇ Curveball	47.2%	81 [108]	5.9 [94]	-52.6 [89]
✦ Slow Curveball				
✱ Knuckleball				
▼ Screwball				

Steven Wright RHP

Born: 08/30/84   Age: 35   Bats: R   Throws: R
Height: 6'2"   Weight: 215   Origin: Round 2, 2006 Draft (#56 overall)

YEAR	TEAM	LVL	AGE	W	L	SV	G	GS	IP	H	HR	BB/9	K/9	K	GB%	BABIP
2017	BOS	MLB	32	1	3	0	5	5	24	40	9	1.9	4.9	13	43%	.365
2018	PAW	AAA	33	0	0	0	5	3	16²	20	0	2.2	4.9	9	48%	.333
2018	BOS	MLB	33	3	1	1	20	4	53²	41	5	4.4	7.0	42	54%	.243
2019	PAW	AAA	34	1	0	0	5	1	9²	6	1	2.8	3.7	4	53%	.172
2019	BOS	MLB	34	0	1	0	6	0	6¹	11	3	5.7	7.1	5	35%	.400
2020	BOS	MLB	35	2	2	0	33	0	35	36	8	2.9	5.3	21	43%	.261

Comparables: George Kontos, Jeff Manship, Fernando Salas

Wright has gone from an intriguing underdog story to an All-Star to an oft-injured arm who can't stay on the mound even when healthy—in the span of about 12 months, he was suspended for PED use and, more seriously, a violation of the league's domestic violence policy. Released by the Red Sox in October, Wright paired that career development with Tommy John surgery, which means the earliest he figures to see another major-league mound is 2021. Once he's healthy, perhaps some team will recall the effectiveness Wright displayed in a limited stint in 2018 and try to use him for some innings on the cheap. But overall, it's tough to find anything the 35-year-old has done on or off the field over the past three years that indicates he should be given additional chances.

YEAR	TEAM	LVL	AGE	WHIP	ERA	DRA	WARP	MPH	FB%	WHF	CSP
2017	BOS	MLB	32	1.88	8.25	8.93	-0.9	87.6	8.2	7.2	48.3
2018	PAW	AAA	33	1.44	3.78	5.91	-0.1				
2018	BOS	MLB	33	1.25	2.68	2.72	1.5	88.0	7.5	10	52.3
2019	PAW	AAA	34	0.93	1.86	3.66	0.2				
2019	BOS	MLB	34	2.37	8.53	7.78	-0.2	83.4	6.1	9.2	52.1
2020	BOS	MLB	35	1.36	5.10	5.28	0.0	86.3	7.4	9.1	50.3

Boston Red Sox 2020

Steven Wright, continued

Pitch Shape vs LHH

Pitch Shape vs RHH

PLAYER COMMENTS WITHOUT GRAPHS

Jackie Bradley Jr. CF
Born: 04/19/90 Age: 30 Bats: L Throws: R
Height: 5'10" Weight: 200 Origin: Round 1, 2011 Draft (#40 overall)

YEAR	TEAM	LVL	AGE	PA	R	2B	3B	HR	RBI	BB	K	SB	CS	AVG/OBP/SLG
2017	BOS	MLB	27	541	58	19	3	17	63	48	124	8	3	.245/.323/.402
2018	BOS	MLB	28	535	76	33	4	13	59	46	137	17	1	.234/.314/.403
2019	BOS	MLB	29	567	69	28	3	21	62	56	155	8	6	.225/.317/.421
2020	BOS	MLB	30	560	61	29	3	19	67	53	157	8	3	.226/.313/.410

Comparables: Ray Lankford, Aaron Hicks, Peter Bourjos

Few things in baseball cause more cognitive dissonance than what the eye test tells you about Bradley's defense and what defensive metrics would have you to believe. For the second year in a row, FRAA hasn't been overly impressed by his defense in center field. But for the seventh straight season, he sure looked like a natural out there en route to yet *another* Gold Glove nomination. Now entering his walk year, Bradley has to view this discrepancy in defensive valuation as a major threat to his future earnings. It's been three years since he's offered a better than league-average bat, and as he enters his age-30 season, it's probably safe to stop waiting for a breakout. If he's still the Gold Glover many think he is, Bradley has plenty to offer as a run-saver and professional down-the-order hitter. If not, we're fast approaching a time when Bradley offers far more name value than actual value.

YEAR	TEAM	LVL	AGE	PA	DRC+	VORP	BABIP	BRR	FRAA	WARP
2017	BOS	MLB	27	541	96	19.3	.294	3.8	CF(132): -7.4	1.3
2018	BOS	MLB	28	535	88	14.9	.299	2.5	CF(135): 6.1, RF(15): 0.3	1.9
2019	BOS	MLB	29	567	86	10.8	.281	0.9	CF(144): 0.9, RF(3): 0.4	1.3
2020	BOS	MLB	30	560	87	13.0	.292	1.8	CF 0	1.3

Cameron Cannon SS

Born: 10/16/97 Age: 22 Bats: R Throws: R
Height: 5'10" Weight: 196 Origin: Round 2, 2019 Draft (#43 overall)

YEAR	TEAM	LVL	AGE	PA	R	2B	3B	HR	RBI	BB	K	SB	CS	AVG/OBP/SLG
2019	LOW	A-	21	180	17	12	0	3	21	12	37	1	0	.205/.289/.335
2020	BOS	MLB	22	251	22	12	1	6	25	14	76	2	1	.204/.260/.343

Comparables: David Adams, Taylor Featherston, Sheldon Neuse

There are other places in the multiverse in which a character named Cameron Cannon is the main protagonist of a series of Young Adult novels, or Brandi Maxxxx's understudy or the new Spider-Man. In our timeline, he's Boston's first selection from the 2019 draft. That fact alone may overstate Cannon's upside—the Sox didn't pick until the second round thanks to luxury tax penalties, and Cannon doesn't have a ton to offer in the way of splashy tools. Still, he's a bat-first middle infielder with plenty of athleticism who scouts think will probably move fairly quickly towards a long-term home at second base. The last time the Sox popped a guy with that profile out of an Arizona school, it worked out okay.

YEAR	TEAM	LVL	AGE	PA	DRC+	VORP	BABIP	BRR	FRAA	WARP
2019	LOW	A-	21	180	101	2.6	.248	0.2	2B(19): 1.8, SS(18): -0.8	0.7
2020	BOS	MLB	22	251	59	-5.3	.274	0.0	SS 0, 2B 0	-0.5

Triston Casas 1B

Born: 01/15/00   Age: 20   Bats: L   Throws: R
Height: 6'4"   Weight: 238   Origin: Round 1, 2018 Draft (#26 overall)

YEAR	TEAM	LVL	AGE	PA	R	2B	3B	HR	RBI	BB	K	SB	CS	AVG/OBP/SLG
2019	GRN	A	19	493	64	25	5	19	78	58	116	3	2	.254/.349/.472
2020	BOS	MLB	20	251	26	12	1	9	30	20	74	3	1	.219/.289/.395

Comparables: Matt Olson, Mike Carp, Trayce Thompson

Boston's first-round pick in 2018, Casas has taken the leap from "best prospect in a terrible system" to "potential legitimate top-100 dude." After his debut professional season was cut short by a torn UCL in his thumb, Casas got off to a very slow start in 2019, hitting just .208/.384/.364 in April. He adjusted as you'd expect a first-round talent would, hitting .264/.363/.469 the rest of the way in Low A en route to being named the Red Sox's Minor League Offensive Player of the Year. Casas has already moved to first base full-time and is a poor bet to contend for future batting titles. But he's got plenty of pop, better makeup than a Sephora outlet and a good idea what he's doing at the plate. "What if Eric Hosmer, but slower" isn't the sexiest ceiling in the world, but it's nothing to shake a stick at, either.

YEAR	TEAM	LVL	AGE	PA	DRC+	VORP	BABIP	BRR	FRAA	WARP
2019	GRN	A	19	493	145	24.1	.300	-0.9	1B(94): -4.7, 3B(8): -1.2	2.1
2020	BOS	MLB	20	251	81	1.6	.282	-0.4	1B -2, 3B 0	0.0

Bobby Dalbec 3B

Born: 06/29/95   Age: 25   Bats: R   Throws: R
Height: 6'4"   Weight: 225   Origin: Round 4, 2016 Draft (#118 overall)

YEAR	TEAM	LVL	AGE	PA	R	2B	3B	HR	RBI	BB	K	SB	CS	AVG/OBP/SLG
2017	RSX	RK	22	32	3	1	0	0	2	5	9	1	0	.259/.375/.296
2017	GRN	A	22	329	48	15	0	13	39	36	123	4	5	.246/.345/.437
2018	SLM	A+	23	419	59	27	2	26	85	60	130	3	1	.256/.372/.573
2018	PME	AA	23	124	14	8	1	6	24	6	46	0	0	.261/.323/.514
2019	PME	AA	24	439	57	15	2	20	57	68	110	6	4	.234/.371/.454
2019	PAW	AAA	24	123	12	4	0	7	16	5	29	0	2	.257/.301/.478
2020	BOS	MLB	25	350	39	17	1	14	45	32	113	1	0	.220/.304/.415

Comparables: Jabari Blash, Josh Bell, Taylor Teagarden

For several seasons now any praise for Dalbec has been balanced with the caveat that he whiffs more than often than the New York Times Op-Ed team. It's true that Dalbec's game will always feature plenty of swing-and-miss, but in 2019 he surprised by cutting back on the Ks to a significant degree. Yes, he still struck out a quarter of the time, but hey, progress is progress. All of Dalbec's other strengths remain. He's a good defender at third and first, has a rocket arm, and will have 40-homer power even if the balls become de-juiced. Mark Reynolds has been the butt of many a joke (as well as the best Baseball Prospectus article of all time), but he's also been in the majors for 12 seasons and counting. Dalbec is close enough and does enough things well that he can reasonably dream of enjoying such a future.

YEAR	TEAM	LVL	AGE	PA	DRC+	VORP	BABIP	BRR	FRAA	WARP
2017	RSX	RK	22	32	62	-0.1	.389	0.7	3B(4): -0.5	0.0
2017	GRN	A	22	329	113	13.2	.383	-2.0	3B(67): -2.3	1.0
2018	SLM	A+	23	419	161	44.2	.318	0.9	3B(91): 5.2, SS(1): 0.0	4.5
2018	PME	AA	23	124	96	7.1	.377	-0.1	3B(18): -3.9, 1B(2): -0.3	-0.2
2019	PME	AA	24	439	151	31.4	.278	-2.2	3B(90): 7.2, 1B(13): 0.9	4.2
2019	PAW	AAA	24	123	83	3.8	.278	0.3	3B(17): 2.0, 1B(11): -1.3	0.2
2020	BOS	MLB	25	350	91	1.1	.296	-0.6	1B -2, 3B 0	0.0

Jeter Downs SS

Born: 07/27/98 Age: 21 Bats: R Throws: R
Height: 5'11" Weight: 180 Origin: Round 1, 2017 Draft (#32 overall)

YEAR	TEAM	LVL	AGE	PA	R	2B	3B	HR	RBI	BB	K	SB	CS	AVG/OBP/SLG
2017	BIL	RK	18	209	31	3	3	6	29	27	32	8	5	.267/.370/.424
2018	DYT	A	19	524	63	23	2	13	47	52	103	37	10	.257/.351/.402
2019	RCU	A+	20	479	78	33	4	19	75	54	97	23	8	.269/.354/.507
2019	TUL	AA	20	56	14	2	0	5	11	6	10	1	0	.333/.429/.688
2020	LAN	MLB	21	251	30	12	1	11	34	20	63	7	3	.236/.306/.445

Comparables: Gavin Lux, Carter Kieboom, Alen Hanson

It's been about five years now since a shortstop named Jeter commanded the attention of the baseball world, but Downs is on a mission to change that, turning more and more heads with every game he plays. Only some guy named Gavin Lux kept him from winning the Minor League Player Of The Year for the Dodgers, following his breakout 2019. Acquired in an unpopular trade at the time due to fan favorite Yasiel Puig being dealt, Downs validated the faith of the Dodgers by showing on-base and power skills in High-A, then flexing his muscles even more in a 12-game stint in Double-A. He ended up posting a 20/20 season on the year and forced his way into Top 100 lists everywhere. While it appears Downs is blocked by Corey Seager and/or Lux, the Dodgers value versatility, and Downs has experience at second base, with enough athleticism to try the outfield. He could force his way into a Dodgers debut, but the most likely scenario at this point is he's dealt within the next couple seasons for an impact player.

YEAR	TEAM	LVL	AGE	PA	DRC+	VORP	BABIP	BRR	FRAA	WARP
2017	BIL	RK	18	209	97	12.8	.288	-1.5	SS(50): -4.5	-0.1
2018	DYT	A	19	524	124	23.2	.306	-1.6	2B(73): -2.9, SS(43): -9.3	1.6
2019	RCU	A+	20	479	127	44.3	.304	4.1	SS(90): -4.0, 2B(10): -1.1	2.9
2019	TUL	AA	20	56	167	7.9	.333	0.8	SS(11): -0.4, 2B(1): 0.0	0.6
2020	LAN	MLB	21	251	96	7.3	.276	0.4	SS -4, 2B -1	0.3

Boston Red Sox 2020

Jarren Duran OF

Born: 09/05/96 Age: 23 Bats: L Throws: R
Height: 6'2" Weight: 200 Origin: Round 7, 2018 Draft (#220 overall)

YEAR	TEAM	LVL	AGE	PA	R	2B	3B	HR	RBI	BB	K	SB	CS	AVG/OBP/SLG
2018	LOW	A-	21	168	28	5	10	2	20	11	26	12	4	.348/.393/.548
2018	GRN	A	21	134	24	9	1	1	15	5	22	12	6	.367/.396/.477
2019	SLM	A+	22	226	49	13	3	4	19	23	44	18	5	.387/.456/.543
2019	PME	AA	22	352	41	11	5	1	19	23	84	28	8	.250/.309/.325
2020	BOS	MLB	23	251	24	11	2	4	24	13	67	11	6	.264/.309/.380

Comparables: Jedd Gyorko, Andrew Stevenson, Eddie Rosario

A seventh-round pick out of Long Beach State in 2018, Duran has emerged in short order as one of the more intriguing prospects on *Planet Earth*. Armed with plus-plus speed, great bat-to-ball ability and *The Reflex*(es) needed to succeed at the plate, Duran rode his skills and a ludicrous BABIP to flirt with a .400 average in High A. After a midseason promotion to Portland, things started to *Come Undone*, but Duran still acquitted himself reasonably well for a dude who was in college about 12 months earlier. Despite the impressive start to his career, there are holes in Duran's game. He's got a *Notorious*-ly weak arm that could limit him to left field, and he offers very little in the way of power at present; he'll have to do most of his damage between the *White Lines*. Still, scouts say Duran is *Hungry (Like The Wolf)* to get better, and if the hit tool ticks up a half-grade we're looking at a potential everyday regular.

YEAR	TEAM	LVL	AGE	PA	DRC+	VORP	BABIP	BRR	FRAA	WARP
2018	LOW	A-	21	168	177	19.6	.406	0.4	2B(20): 4.9, CF(15): 0.1	2.2
2018	GRN	A	21	134	167	12.2	.438	1.6	RF(30): 0.0	1.3
2019	SLM	A+	22	226	201	30.5	.480	3.4	CF(50): 0.2	3.3
2019	PME	AA	22	352	76	9.9	.335	5.1	CF(79): -3.3	0.5
2020	BOS	MLB	23	251	81	3.1	.355	1.1	CF -1, RF 0	0.2

Gilberto Jimenez OF

Born: 07/08/00 Age: 19 Bats: B Throws: R
Height: 5'11" Weight: 160 Origin: International Free Agent, 2017

YEAR	TEAM	LVL	AGE	PA	R	2B	3B	HR	RBI	BB	K	SB	CS	AVG/OBP/SLG
2018	DRS	RK	17	284	42	10	8	0	22	19	40	16	14	.319/.384/.420
2019	LOW	A-	18	254	35	11	3	3	19	13	38	14	6	.359/.393/.470
2020	BOS	MLB	19	251	23	11	2	3	23	15	57	6	5	.271/.321/.369

Comparables: Victor Robles, Harold Ramírez, Enrique Hernández

The Red Sox's farm system is perhaps less desolate than a season ago, but it's still fairly bereft of high-upside talent. Jimenez serves as an exception. A blazingly fast center fielder who the Sox signed out of the Dominican as an IFA in 2017, Jimenez made quick work of the New York-Penn League as an 18-year-old. While power isn't a part of his game, he's a potential plus switch-hitter who's already showing impressive bat-to-ball skills from the left side despite just starting to hit from there in 2017. Defensively, speed is Jimenez's primary calling card, but he also offers above-average arm strength, giving him all the ingredients of a potential impact center fielder. If you're counting at home, that's four average-or-better tools Jimenez flashes at present, which a year ago may have been more than the rest of Boston's farm offered collectively. He's another good season away from entering the national prospect consciousness.

YEAR	TEAM	LVL	AGE	PA	DRC+	VORP	BABIP	BRR	FRAA	WARP
2018	DRS	RK	17	284	146	25.1	.378	-1.0	CF(64): 3.4	2.5
2019	LOW	A-	18	254	191	30.7	.413	1.2	CF(57): -9.8, RF(1): -0.1	1.9
2020	BOS	MLB	19	251	86	3.3	.349	-0.2	CF -3, RF 0	0.0

Dustin Pedroia 2B

Born: 08/17/83   Age: 36   Bats: R   Throws: R
Height: 5'9"   Weight: 175   Origin: Round 2, 2004 Draft (#65 overall)

YEAR	TEAM	LVL	AGE	PA	R	2B	3B	HR	RBI	BB	K	SB	CS	AVG/OBP/SLG
2017	BOS	MLB	33	463	46	19	0	7	62	49	48	4	3	.293/.369/.392
2018	BOS	MLB	34	13	1	0	0	0	0	2	1	0	0	.091/.231/.091
2019	BOS	MLB	35	21	1	0	0	0	1	1	2	0	0	.100/.143/.100
2020	*BOS*	*MLB*	*36*	*35*	*3*	*2*	*0*	*1*	*3*	*3*	*5*	*0*	*0*	*.255/.321/.371*

Comparables: Adam Kennedy, Steve Sax, Ramon Martinez

At its best, baseball rewards perseverance, celebrates its unique talents and sends its heroes out with honor and dignity. At its worst, the game is unforgiving and cruel, forcing its stars to limp undignified to the finish line. Pedroia has now played in just nine games over the last two seasons because of his left knee. The experimental "cartilage restoration procedure" he had during the 2017-2018 offseason has not worked, or at least not well enough to withstand the rigors that come with being a professional athlete. At a May press conference, Pedroia admitted as such for the first time—perhaps as much to himself as to the rest of us—and while he's stopped short of officially retiring to date, there's a good chance he will have by the time this book is in your hands. That's a damn shame for many reasons, not least of which because it means Pedroia, long one of the game's best pure hitters when healthy, will finish with a career batting average of .299. In reality, his legacy is already set—a three-time World Series winner, MVP and franchise icon whose serious bid for Hall-of-Fame consideration ended four or five years ago—but it's sad the game won't provide him with a more poetic ending. Few players of his generation have loved baseball quite so obviously as Pedroia has, but in the end it's proving it can't love him back.

YEAR	TEAM	LVL	AGE	PA	DRC+	VORP	BABIP	BRR	FRAA	WARP
2017	BOS	MLB	33	463	109	9.2	.315	-5.7	2B(98): -0.1	1.3
2018	BOS	MLB	34	13	97	-1.3	.100	-0.1	2B(3): -0.4	0.0
2019	BOS	MLB	35	21	87	0.1	.111	-0.1	2B(4): -0.2	0.0
2020	*BOS*	*MLB*	*36*	*35*	*86*	*0.5*	*.291*	*-0.2*	*2B 0*	*0.1*

Connor Wong C

Born: 05/19/96   Age: 24   Bats: R   Throws: R
Height: 6'1"   Weight: 181   Origin: Round 3, 2017 Draft (#100 overall)

YEAR	TEAM	LVL	AGE	PA	R	2B	3B	HR	RBI	BB	K	SB	CS	AVG/OBP/SLG
2017	GRL	A	21	107	19	6	0	5	18	7	26	1	1	.278/.336/.495
2018	RCU	A+	22	431	64	20	2	19	60	38	138	6	2	.269/.350/.480
2019	RCU	A+	23	302	39	15	6	15	51	21	93	9	2	.245/.306/.507
2019	TUL	AA	23	163	17	9	1	9	31	11	50	2	1	.349/.393/.604
2020	LAN	MLB	24	251	25	12	1	9	30	15	91	1	0	.226/.281/.400

Comparables: Xavier Scruggs, Eric Haase, Jamie Romak

Buried behind the likes of Austin Barnes, Will Smith, Keibert Ruiz and even Diego Cartaya is Wong, who has flown under the radar and has stealthily turned himself into a

YEAR	TEAM	P. COUNT	FRM RUNS	BLK RUNS	THRW RUNS	TOT RUNS
2019	TUL	3251	-0.8	0.0	1.3	0.5
2020	LAN	7805	-3.3	-0.5	1.1	-2.8

legitimate prospect. An athletic backstop that played shortstop in college and can play both second and third, Wong handled advanced pitching well in 2019 and bumped his stock significantly by doing so. He has pop, but it comes along with a 31 percent strikeout rate that has to improve if he wants to take the next step. To Wong's credit, he has been working on a bat path that will generate more consistent contact, and if it sticks then the Dodgers may envision him as a unique type of super-utility player.

YEAR	TEAM	LVL	AGE	PA	DRC+	VORP	BABIP	BRR	FRAA	WARP
2017	GRL	A	21	107	125	7.4	.328	0.0	C(27): 0.2	0.8
2018	RCU	A+	22	431	113	27.8	.372	0.9	C(71): 0.7, 2B(11): -0.5	2.4
2019	RCU	A+	23	302	102	22.6	.310	1.3	C(59): 0.7, 2B(10): 1.3	1.7
2019	TUL	AA	23	163	163	18.1	.467	0.3	C(23): 0.1, 3B(10): -0.8	1.5
2020	LAN	MLB	24	251	77	0.2	.331	-0.2	C -3, 2B 0	-0.2

Durbin Feltman RHP

Born: 04/18/97   Age: 23   Bats: R   Throws: R
Height: 6'0"   Weight: 205   Origin: Round 3, 2018 Draft (#100 overall)

YEAR	TEAM	LVL	AGE	W	L	SV	G	GS	IP	H	HR	BB/9	K/9	K	GB%	BABIP
2018	GRN	A	21	0	1	3	7	0	7	6	0	1.3	18.0	14	43%	.429
2018	SLM	A+	21	1	0	1	11	0	12¹	12	0	2.9	10.9	15	58%	.364
2019	PME	AA	22	2	3	5	43	0	51¹	42	8	5.4	9.5	54	43%	.266
2020	BOS	MLB	23	2	2	0	33	0	35	35	6	3.7	8.7	34	41%	.302

Comparables: Shawn Armstrong, Evan Phillips, Trevor Gott

Coming out of the draft in 2018, Feltman was considered about as safe a reliever prospect as could be. For the umpteenth time, "safe reliever prospect" has turned out to be quite the oxymoron. Feltman struggled mightily in Double-A, coughing up walks and homers at such a rate that one wonders if he was performing some sort of masochistic tribute to late-career Daniel Bard. Feltman still owns the type of high-velocity fastball/wipeout slider combo that many of the game's high-leverage relievers feature, but he'll need to hit the strike zone far more often if he wants a chance at deploying said weapons in Boston.

YEAR	TEAM	LVL	AGE	WHIP	ERA	DRA	WARP	MPH	FB%	WHF	CSP
2018	GRN	A	21	1.00	2.57	2.65	0.2				
2018	SLM	A+	21	1.30	2.19	3.68	0.2				
2019	PME	AA	22	1.42	5.26	5.14	-0.3				
2020	BOS	MLB	23	1.41	4.72	4.87	0.1				

Jay Groome   LHP

Born: 08/23/98   Age: 21   Bats: L   Throws: L
Height: 6'6"   Weight: 220   Origin: Round 1, 2016 Draft (#12 overall)

YEAR	TEAM	LVL	AGE	W	L	SV	G	GS	IP	H	HR	BB/9	K/9	K	GB%	BABIP
2017	LOW	A-	18	0	2	0	3	3	11	5	0	4.1	11.5	14	58%	.208
2017	GRN	A	18	3	7	0	11	11	44[1]	44	6	5.1	11.8	58	55%	.355
2020	BOS	MLB	21	2	2	0	33	0	35	35	6	4.1	9.0	35	47%	.304

Comparables: Lewis Thorpe, Jordan Lyles, Mike Soroka

Folks, we haven't seen a Groome get abandoned like this since *The Princess Bride*. Our protagonist was a consensus top-three pitcher in the 2016 draft and top-100 prospect in the game as recently as 2017. But since Groome has been largely out of sight, out of mind for 15 months as he recovered from Tommy John surgery, it seems as though his prospect luster has faded. It's entirely possible that Groome will serve as example number 23,542 as to why the TINSTAAPP acronym was invented. It's also possible that Groome, who looked great once he climbed back on a mound in August, is about to remind us all why he generated so many Jon Lester comps to begin with.

YEAR	TEAM	LVL	AGE	WHIP	ERA	DRA	WARP	MPH	FB%	WHF	CSP
2017	LOW	A-	18	0.91	1.64	2.65	0.3				
2017	GRN	A	18	1.56	6.70	4.49	0.4				
2020	BOS	MLB	21	1.47	4.97	5.06	0.1				

Tanner Houck RHP

Born: 06/29/96 Age: 24 Bats: R Throws: R
Height: 6'4" Weight: 210 Origin: Round 1, 2017 Draft (#24 overall)

YEAR	TEAM	LVL	AGE	W	L	SV	G	GS	IP	H	HR	BB/9	K/9	K	GB%	BABIP
2017	LOW	A-	21	0	3	0	10	10	22^1	21	0	3.2	10.1	25	49%	.333
2018	SLM	A+	22	7	11	0	23	23	119	110	11	4.5	8.4	111	50%	.298
2019	PME	AA	23	8	6	0	17	15	82^2	86	4	3.5	8.7	80	50%	.346
2019	PAW	AAA	23	0	0	1	16	2	25	19	3	5.0	9.7	27	48%	.250
2020	BOS	MLB	24	1	1	0	3	3	15	14	2	4.0	7.7	12	46%	.292

Comparables: Reed Garrett, Hansel Robles, Corey Kluber

Houck was a first-round pick back in 2017 and that comes with certain expectations, but if you're waiting for him to front a rotation some day it's time to recalibrate. Houck's lack of a reliable third pitch and spotty command are likely to preclude him from dominating as a starter at the next level, and may prevent him from starting there at all. The good news? Houck's fastball/slider combo can miss major-league bats right now, and if that third pitch ever does click, he's got the frame and athleticism to soak up lots of innings. Houck mostly pitched in relief after a promotion to Pawtucket but was featured as a starter in the AFL, so some ambiguity as to his future role remains. For 2020, it's easiest to envision him contributing out of the bullpen with the Red Sox, even if he's only used against righties early in his career. In other words, prepare yourself for lots of "Houck: A ROOGY" jokes next June.

YEAR	TEAM	LVL	AGE	WHIP	ERA	DRA	WARP	MPH	FB%	WHF	CSP
2017	LOW	A-	21	1.30	3.63	4.91	0.1				
2018	SLM	A+	22	1.43	4.24	4.96	0.5				
2019	PME	AA	23	1.43	4.25	5.45	-0.5				
2019	PAW	AAA	23	1.32	3.24	3.52	0.7				
2020	BOS	MLB	24	1.44	4.85	4.88	0.1				

Bryan Mata   RHP

Born: 05/03/99   Age: 21   Bats: R   Throws: R
Height: 6'3"   Weight: 160   Origin: International Free Agent, 2016

YEAR	TEAM	LVL	AGE	W	L	SV	G	GS	IP	H	HR	BB/9	K/9	K	GB%	BABIP
2017	GRN	A	18	5	6	0	17	17	77	75	3	3.0	8.6	74	53%	.333
2018	SLM	A+	19	6	3	0	17	17	72	58	1	7.2	7.6	61	59%	.292
2019	SLM	A+	20	3	1	0	10	10	51^1	38	1	3.2	9.1	52	67%	.268
2019	PME	AA	20	4	6	0	11	11	53^2	54	6	4.0	9.9	59	54%	.340
2020	BOS	MLB	21	2	2	0	33	0	35	34	5	3.7	7.9	31	47%	.292

Comparables: Carlos Martínez, Junior Fernandez, David Holmberg

To be fair to Mata, he's always been kinda young for his levels. Unfortunately, he's also always been kinda bad for his levels. Ok, that's not *quite* true. Mata was dominant in his half-season of repeat work at High A, but following a promotion to Portland the hard-throwing righty's impressive stuff didn't lead to impressive results. For the most part, that's been the story of Mata's career: aggressive assignments, promising scouting reports and lackluster box scores. It seems as though the Red Sox are still grooming Mata as a potential mid-rotation starter, but he pitched out of the bullpen in the AFL and some scouts think his future may lie in relief, where his mid-90s fastball and power slider/curve figure to miss bats. Either way, history tells us Mata won't be young forever, and it's time for his results to start matching his talent.

YEAR	TEAM	LVL	AGE	WHIP	ERA	DRA	WARP	MPH	FB%	WHF	CSP
2017	GRN	A	18	1.31	3.74	4.67	0.5				
2018	SLM	A+	19	1.61	3.50	5.71	-0.3				
2019	SLM	A+	20	1.09	1.75	3.68	0.8				
2019	PME	AA	20	1.45	5.03	5.42	-0.3				
2020	BOS	MLB	21	1.39	4.55	4.68	0.2				

Boston Red Sox 2020

Noah Song   RHP
Born: 05/28/97   Age: 23   Bats: R   Throws: R
Height: 6'4"   Weight: 200   Origin: Round 4, 2019 Draft (#137 overall)

YEAR	TEAM	LVL	AGE	W	L	SV	G	GS	IP	H	HR	BB/9	K/9	K	GB%	BABIP
2019	LOW	A-	22	0	0	0	7	7	17	10	0	2.6	10.1	19	42%	.244
2020	BOS	MLB	23	2	2	0	33	0	35	35	5	3.5	7.9	31	40%	.293

Comparables: Troy Scribner, Jesse Hahn, Daniel Ponce de Leon

You might not find a more intriguing prospect than Song, who the Red Sox popped in the fourth round for a cool $100,000 in last year's draft. Not just because he went from relative unknown to a Golden Spikes Award finalist, nor because on talent alone Song may be the best pitching prospect in Boston's system, but because Song was drafted out of the Naval Academy. That muddles Song's immediate future, as it's equally plausible he could miss the next five years fulfilling his military service commitment as it is he could petition to serve in the reserves after two years, or be granted a waiver that allows him to play baseball full-time. On the mound, Song features a mid-90s fastball, a potent slider and a developing changeup. Add that to his ideal pitcher's build and you've got the ingredients of a solid mid-rotation starter. It's anyone's guess as to when and if Song will be allowed to use those talents in the minors, but at the end of the day we shouldn't be surprised that a guy named "Noah Song" figures to have an interesting career arc.

YEAR	TEAM	LVL	AGE	WHIP	ERA	DRA	WARP	MPH	FB%	WHF	CSP
2019	LOW	A-	22	0.88	1.06	2.49	0.5				
2020	BOS	MLB	23	1.39	4.52	4.68	0.2				

Thad Ward RHP

Born: 01/16/97   Age: 23   Bats: R   Throws: R
Height: 6'3"   Weight: 182   Origin: Round 5, 2018 Draft (#160 overall)

YEAR	TEAM	LVL	AGE	W	L	SV	G	GS	IP	H	HR	BB/9	K/9	K	GB%	BABIP
2018	LOW	A-	21	0	3	0	11	11	31	33	2	3.5	7.8	27	54%	.337
2019	GRN	A	22	5	2	0	13	13	72¹	51	2	3.1	10.8	87	48%	.280
2019	SLM	A+	22	3	3	0	12	12	54	38	4	5.3	11.7	70	48%	.296
2020	BOS	MLB	23	2	2	0	33	0	35	35	5	4.2	9.3	36	45%	.309

Comparables: Parker Bridwell, Dinelson Lamet, Tyler Thornburg

Few systems in baseball were in as much need of a breakout arm as Boston, and Ward obliged. A fifth-round pick by the Sox in 2018, Ward dominated in his first full professional season between Greenville and Salem, including a stretch from May 14 through June 6 in which he did not allow an earned run. Ward has always had a funky, three-quarters delivery that makes his pitches hard to pick up, but the real reason for his ascension may be a new cutter, which Ward used to follow the time-honored South Carolina tradition of marginalizing lefties. Positive developments aside, it's worth pointing out that Ward was old for his levels and awfully wild, especially after he got the bump to High A. A test against more advanced hitters should tell us whether Ward is a flash-in-the-pan or on the path toward becoming Boston's first good homegrown starter in what feels like several decades.

YEAR	TEAM	LVL	AGE	WHIP	ERA	DRA	WARP	MPH	FB%	WHF	CSP
2018	LOW	A-	21	1.45	3.77	5.89	-0.2				
2019	GRN	A	22	1.05	1.99	3.25	1.7				
2019	SLM	A+	22	1.30	2.33	4.35	0.5				
2020	BOS	MLB	23	1.47	4.99	4.96	0.1				

Boston Red Sox 2020

LINEOUTS

Hitters

HITTER	POS	TEAM	LVL	AGE	PA	R	2B	3B	HR	RBI	BB	K	SB	CS	AVG/OBP/SLG	DRC+	WARP
Jonathan Arauz	SS	CCH	AA	20	119	12	3	2	3	13	10	19	1	1	.241/.311/.389	118	0.4
	SS	BCA	A+	20	354	41	19	0	8	42	30	69	5	4	.252/.322/.388	111	1.3
Rusney Castillo	OF	PAW	AAA	31	493	63	25	1	17	64	25	63	5	9	.278/.321/.448	102	1.3
Juan Centeno	C	BOS	MLB	29	18	0	0	0	0	2	2	2	1	0	.133/.278/.133	90	-0.1
	C	PAW	AAA	29	301	27	15	0	4	40	24	47	2	0	.248/.321/.350	84	-1.6
C.J. Chatham	SS	PAW	AAA	24	91	11	5	0	2	10	4	21	0	0	.302/.330/.430	109	0.4
	SS	PME	AA	24	376	39	26	1	3	36	18	66	7	1	.297/.333/.403	126	2.3
Nick Decker	OF	LOW	A-	19	197	23	10	5	6	25	21	59	4	5	.247/.328/.471	121	0.4
Danny Diaz	3B	RSX	Rk	18	113	15	11	0	1	12	5	30	0	0	.210/.257/.343	70	-0.1
Tyler Esplin	OF	GRN	A	19	436	52	26	3	5	43	40	107	6	3	.253/.326/.375	111	0.6
Antoni Flores	SS	LOW	A-	18	208	14	4	1	0	12	25	59	1	3	.193/.293/.227	84	0.8
Gorkys Hernandez	CF	PAW	AAA	31	504	75	14	3	16	53	62	146	20	6	.219/.319/.377	77	0.1
	CF	BOS	MLB	31	57	5	1	2	0	2	5	14	1	0	.143/.218/.245	71	0.0
Brandon Howlett	3B	GRN	A	19	465	48	23	1	8	35	56	144	1	5	.231/.341/.356	110	0.4
Tzu-Wei Lin	2B	BOS	MLB	25	22	3	2	0	0	1	2	6	1	1	.200/.273/.300	71	0.0
	2B	PAW	AAA	25	250	30	11	1	4	22	21	58	6	2	.246/.308/.357	84	1.2
Nick Longhi	LF	LOU	AAA	23	424	51	28	3	12	51	30	102	0	1	.283/.336/.463	103	0.9
Matthew Lugo	SS	RSX	Rk	18	157	19	5	1	1	12	15	36	3	0	.257/.342/.331	125	1.2
Jhon Nunez	C	PME	AA	24	233	26	11	1	5	21	13	39	5	3	.280/.333/.412	116	1.1
Josh Ockimey	1B	PAW	AAA	23	468	64	17	2	25	57	82	139	0	2	.204/.353/.459	113	0.6
Austin Rei	C	PME	AA	25	90	4	5	0	1	9	6	29	0	0	.157/.213/.253	40	-0.2
Marcus Wilson	OF	SLM	A+	22	167	26	12	1	8	29	18	47	4	3	.342/.413/.603	212	1.9
	OF	PME	AA	22	238	35	14	0	8	22	28	82	6	0	.223/.319/.408	101	0.3
	OF	WTN	AA	22	40	4	2	1	2	7	5	13	3	1	.235/.350/.529	121	0.2

Good news: **Jonathan Arauz** posted a career-best OPS in 2019. Bad news: It was .707. The glove is nice, though, and the world is always ready for another glove-first shortstop. ⓧ Forgotten outfielder **Rusney Castillo** continues to prove that he's too good for Triple-A, but too expensive for the majors. In exercising his player option for 2020, Castillo has ensured that he'll get $13.5 million, but also that he'll be spending another full season in Pawtucket. ⓧ Probably the only thing you need to know about career backup catcher **Juan Centeno** at this point is that the Red Sox didn't think he'd be an upgrade over Sandy León. ⓧ Future backup infielder **C.J. Chatham** has proven definitively in both Portland and Pawtucket that he can hit for decent averages and zero power. By his sixth major-league game, he'll have been compared to Brock Holt four thousand times. ⓧ 2018 second-round pick **Nick Decker** may only look like a potential fourth outfielder with pop, but as a cold-weather prep bat we can get away with projecting more for at least another five or six seasons. ⓧ Potential slugging third baseman **Danny Diaz** crushed the DSL but got crushed by the GCL, which means he's SOL if he wanted to appear on any top prospect lists this offseason. ⚾ **Jhonathan Diaz** signed for $1.5 million dollars as an international free agent. The teenage outfielder receives high marks for speed and defense with potential to add with the bat. ⚾ This is probably the first time you've heard of potential lefty slugger **Tyler Esplin**, but if he wasn't full of promise why would Boston have already named that big area right by the Charles River after him? ⚾ Promising teenage shortstop prospect **Antoni Flores** faced lots of older competition as an 18-year-old in the New York-Penn League. Even so, he was probably hoping to hit above the Mendoza Line. ⚾ It's unfortunate that as soon as **Gorkys Hernández** learned a new trick—hitting for power—baseball made it so that the rest of the world could easily follow suit. As such, Hernández remains more remarkable for his first name than for anything he can do on the diamond. ⚾ If third base prospect **Brandon Howlett** is going to insist on developing into a Three True Outcomes guy, he'd better increase the frequency with which he provides the best of the outcome trio. ⚾ In missing much of 2019 with a litany of injuries, speedy utility man **Tzu-Wei Lin** took his role as Brock Holt's understudy a bit too literally. ⚾ You could describe **Nick Longhi**'s seven years in the minors with a .736 OPS at unimportant defensive positions as a slow burn—or, you could say Longhi's playing days will soon journey into night. Either way. ⚾ He may have been Boston's second-round pick, but it's easy to argue that speedy shortstop prospect **Matthew Lugo** was the highest-upside hitter they popped in the 2019 draft. Red Sox fans can relax: he's not related to Julio. ⚾ **Jhon Nunez** is a small, athletic backstop with a good arm who should be thrilled if he has Juan Centeno's career. ⚾ Three True Outcomes lord **Josh Ockimey** keeps proving he can really hit for power and can't really do much else as he climbs the ladder. ⚾ **Austin Rei** (pronounced "Ray") wasn't in last year's book, when his PECOTA comparable was Petey Paramore. Of course, Paramore is also the name of a band signed to the Fueled by Ramen label. These facts are as loosely connected as the Red Sox will be to the playoff race if Rei gets significant burn. ⚾ Acquired for the low, low price of one Blake Swihart last April, **Marcus Wilson** made the 40-man roster this past offseason thanks to his speed and defense.

Boston Red Sox 2020

Pitchers

PITCHER	TEAM	LVL	AGE	W	L	SV	G	GS	IP	H	HR	BB/9	K/9	K	GB%	WHIP	ERA	DRA	WARP
Yoan Aybar	GRN	A	21	1	3	0	40	0	51^2	34	1	7.0	11.7	67	53%	1.43	4.88	4.37	0.3
Kyle Hart	PME	AA	26	3	6	0	9	9	55^2	39	3	2.7	9.7	60	39%	1.01	2.91	3.58	0.9
	PAW	AAA	26	9	7	0	18	15	100^1	91	8	3.2	7.2	80	41%	1.27	3.86	4.38	2.2
Brian Johnson	PME	AA	28	0	1	0	3	2	6	11	1	4.5	10.5	7	44%	2.33	10.50	7.91	-0.2
	PAW	AAA	28	1	0	0	6	3	14^2	13	1	4.9	11.7	19	48%	1.43	3.68	4.71	0.3
	BOS	MLB	28	1	3	0	21	7	40^1	53	6	5.1	6.9	31	43%	1.88	6.02	8.15	-1.1
Travis Lakins	PAW	AAA	25	3	4	6	40	1	45	46	4	4.6	8.4	42	42%	1.53	4.60	5.26	0.4
	BOS	MLB	25	0	1	0	16	3	23^1	23	1	3.9	6.9	18	48%	1.41	3.86	6.06	-0.2
Chris Mazza	BIN	AA	29	0	2	0	4	4	23^2	26	0	3.0	8.0	21	51%	1.44	3.42	5.80	-0.2
	SYR	AAA	29	3	3	0	14	13	76	65	6	2.1	7.3	62	59%	1.09	3.67	2.78	2.9
	NYN	MLB	29	1	1	0	9	0	16^1	21	0	2.8	6.1	11	41%	1.59	5.51	7.73	-0.4
Jenrry Mejia	LOW	A-	29	0	1	1	6	0	6^1	7	1	1.4	11.4	8	63%	1.26	4.26	3.91	0.1
	PAW	AAA	29	2	7	7	42	0	48	52	9	3.0	9.2	49	42%	1.42	6.38	5.27	0.4
Chris Murphy	LOW	A-	21	0	1	0	10	10	33^1	23	1	1.9	9.2	34	45%	0.90	1.08	3.40	0.7
Bobby Poyner	PAW	AAA	26	2	5	6	43	1	57^1	47	9	4.2	11.0	70	22%	1.29	3.77	3.76	1.4
	BOS	MLB	26	0	1	0	13	1	11^2	10	2	3.9	8.5	11	28%	1.29	6.94	6.55	-0.1
Aldo Ramirez	LOW	A-	18	2	3	0	14	13	61^2	59	5	2.3	9.2	63	48%	1.22	3.94	4.78	0.3
Erasmo Ramirez	PAW	AAA	29	6	8	0	27	24	125^1	125	18	3.1	6.8	95	48%	1.34	4.74	4.61	2.5
	BOS	MLB	29	0	0	0	1	0	3	4	2	3.0	3.0	1	50%	1.67	12.00	7.01	-0.1
Denyi Reyes	PME	AA	22	8	12	0	26	26	151^1	142	14	2.2	6.9	116	33%	1.18	4.16	4.52	0.8
Michael Shawaryn	PAW	AAA	24	1	2	0	26	14	89^2	76	13	4.9	7.6	76	43%	1.39	4.52	4.40	1.9
	BOS	MLB	24	0	0	0	14	0	20^1	26	5	5.8	12.8	29	32%	1.92	9.74	6.94	-0.3
Ryan Weber	PAW	AAA	28	1	5	0	16	16	78	86	9	2.9	7.3	63	55%	1.42	4.50	4.90	1.4
	BOS	MLB	28	2	4	0	18	3	40^2	48	5	1.8	6.4	29	50%	1.38	5.09	4.98	0.2
Ryan Zeferjahn	LOW	A-	21	0	2	0	12	12	22	24	2	4.9	12.7	31	40%	1.64	4.50	6.45	-0.3

Converted outfielder **Yoan Aybar** has relatively little idea where the ball is going when he releases it, but as an athletic lefty who can hit the mid-90s with his fastball, he'll be given plenty of time to figure it out. ⓧ Now that he's reached Pawtucket, it's time for 27-year-old potential LOOGY **Kyle Hart** to take a big sip out of his "I love getting pulled after just one important batter" mug and read about the upcoming rule changes... ⓧ Whether used as a starter or in relief, former first-rounder **Brian Johnson** was wholly ineffective even by his relatively modest standards. It's clear at this point he does not belong on a first-division club, which made him a perfect fit for the 2019 Red Sox. ⓧ Don't let his ERA fool you; righty **Travis Lakins** walked too many hitters, allowed too many hits and missed too few bats in his first MLB stint. In Boston bullpen terms, his results may scream "Marcus Walden," but his performance more suggests "Colten Brewer." ⚾ After bouncing around the minors for his entire career, **Chris Mazza** finally got the call-up to the big leagues and it did not go well. His stuff was mostly underwhelming, but his story (including a stopover in the Pacific Association of *The Only Rule Is It Has To Work* fame) was anything but. ⚾ We'll say this about **Jenrry Mejia**'s ill-fated comeback; if he's still taking PEDs, he should get his money back for the whole P and E parts. ⚾ A sixth-rounder who shares a name with 30 percent of the population of South Boston, **Chris Murphy** is left-handed enough to warrant some attention as a potential big league reliever. ⚾ Quad-A LOOGY **Bobby Poyner** continued to miss bats in Pawtucket, but his brief major-league stints have proven he's got about as much upside as penny stocks. ⚾ Mexican right-hander **Aldo Ramirez** might not love getting the standard "back-end starting pitcher prospect" tag, but if the (accessibly-priced) shoe fits… ⚾ **Erasmo Ramírez** kept his consecutive years appearing in the majors streak alive on April 16, when he allowed four earned runs in three innings against the Yankees. The rest is better left unsaid. ⚾ What if Dennys Reyes ate at Denny's less often? He might look something like righty **Denyi Reyes**, who makes up for what he lacks in velocity, upside and girth with impressive command and control. ⚾ Fire-hydrant-shaped right-hander **Michael Shawaryn** missed lots of bats in his first 20 major-league innings. He found lots of them too en route to surrendering more than an earned run per inning. ⚾ Once-promising sidewinder **Carson Smith** had one of the best 2019 seasons among all Red Sox relievers, as he was released by the team in mid-June while still recovering from labrum surgery. ⚾ There are lots of ways to say "the 2019 Red Sox had a mediocre bullpen," but none are quite so succinct as "**Ryan Weber** set a new career-high in innings pitched." ⚾ Boston's third-round pick in the 2019 draft, **Ryan Zeferjahn** is your typical hard-throwing righty with a good fastball and few other discernible skills. Let's hope he makes it to the bigs, because we need to hear Jerry Remy try to pronounce his name (Ze-fuh-jun?).

Red Sox Prospects

The State of the System
The 2019 draft class gave the system a much needed injection of talent, but the Sox still lack for impact prospects.

The Top Ten

1 Triston Casas   1B OFP: 55 ETA: Late 2022
Born: 01/15/00   Age: 20   Bats: L   Throws: R   Height: 6'4"   Weight: 238
Origin: Round 1, 2018 Draft (#26 overall)

The Report: It was an up-and-down year for the 2018 first-rounder. Casas showed off his plus power tool to the tune of 19 home runs and 25 doubles, but the extra-base pop came in spurts. His power stroke is best utilized when he shoots the ball to the left-center field gap. However, he would fall into spells where he would try to pull everything, exacerbating his swing-and-miss tendencies and raising questions about the hit tool projection. But even with those concerns, Casas still has the potential to flirt with 40 home runs on a yearly basis, due to his strength and quick bat. His load is very quiet, employing a minimal leg kick and no movement in his upper half, meaning he only needs a change to his approach and not an overhaul of the swing mechanics. Defensively Casas made positive strides throughout the season. It isn't always smooth at first base, but he possesses the basic tools to be an average fielder. His backhand impressed me on multiple occasions. His best attribute in the field is his plus arm. What keeps me optimistic about Casas is his makeup. From multiple sources, he is teachable, a competitor and someone who puts in the extra work–all traits that will help him reach his potential.

Variance: Medium. His power tool and ability to play an average first base gives Casas a fairly high floor. But his full potential in the bigs hinges on improvements to his approach, which will turn him from an average player into a potential All-Star.

Ben Carsley's Fantasy Take: It's always fun when the best guy in a system is a first baseman in the low minors! I actually like Casas quite a bit for a player with his profile; it's just not a terribly enticing fantasy skill set. The dream is Casas improves his approach and turns into a .270/30/100-type on the regular. There's plenty of value in that, of course, but a) it's gonna come at first base and b) please remember that's indicative of Casas' upside, and not a promise of what's to come. It's awfully early to be talking about rankings, but Casas strikes me as the type of dude who'll get knocked off our top-101 in favor of toolsier teenagers, stuck in the dreaded "honorable mentions" until he's closer to the bigs. That still makes him worth rostering in most dynasty leagues, though.

2. Noah Song   RHP   OFP: 55   ETA: ??
Born: 05/28/97   Age: 23   Bats: R   Throws: R   Height: 6'4"   Weight: 200
Origin: Round 4, 2019 Draft (#137 overall)

The Report: Song has one of the most unusual backgrounds of any prospect in recent memory, as a top pitching prospect currently facing an obligation to serve at least two years in the armed forces. He pitched collegiately at the Naval Academy and stayed until graduation; the Red Sox drafted him in the fourth round last summer despite an unclear future in baseball. After Song played for Team USA in Olympic qualifying last fall, he sought a waiver to postpone his military commitment to the end of his pro career. As of press time, the waiver has not been granted, and it is increasingly likely that he will miss most or all of the 2020 and 2021 seasons while serving as a Naval flight officer.

If Song were free and clear from those military commitments, he'd rank first on this list and would've made the 101. It's a testament to his talent that he still ranks where he does even building in the risk that he's iced for several years. In terms of baseball functionality, he's an advanced first-round talent college arm with big stuff, the type of player who is a real boon to the system. He manipulates a low-to-mid-90s fastball with aplomb, touching 98 as a starter and a tick or two higher in relief. His plus slider was far too much for New York-Penn League hitters after the draft, and he mixes in a change and curve as well. He could move quickly as an impact starter or reliever... if only he gets a chance to pitch.

Variance: Unusual, because of the risk that he'll be unavailable for most or all of the early-2020s.

Ben Carsley's Fantasy Take: How is this for a hot take: until we have a better understanding of how long his military commitment will keep him from the mound, Song shouldn't be owned at all. Yes, at all. Consider how much risk the average starting pitcher prospect comes with. Now add in the unique circumstances surrounding Song's career, and you can see how I'd come to that conclusion. I understand that Song is probably a top-150 guy on talent alone, but the risk-to-reward payoff is just much, much too high for me. Unless my league rosters ~300-plus prospects—at which point I have much bigger problems—I'm letting Song serve as someone else's gamble.

3. Bobby Dalbec   3B   OFP: 55   ETA: Second half 2020
Born: 06/29/95   Age: 25   Bats: R   Throws: R   Height: 6'4"   Weight: 225
Origin: Round 4, 2016 Draft (#118 overall)

The Report: Shortly after Dalbec was drafted, some doofus suggested his best shot at the major leagues might come with a move back to the mound. The K-rates continue to be high, but they have improved as Dalbec has moved up the minor-league ladder, and he's gotten enough of his 70 raw power into games to perhaps fit as the kind of Three True Outcomes slugger that's in vogue in 2019 (and probably 2020) baseball. The power comes from length and leverage, and there's some stiffness to the swing, but Dalbec is a big, strong human, and if he can make enough good contact, the slash line will take care of itself. The Red Sox ran this profile in 2019 with Michael Chavis, and it's a similar set of strengths and weaknesses, although Dalbec is a little bit better defensively at the hot corner, with—as you'd expect—a much better arm. But the margins for this profile are thin, as Chavis found out last year. As always the line between Pete Alonso and C.J. Cron is slim for the R/R corner mashers.

Variance: Medium. He might just be 2019 Michael Chavis instead.

Ben Carsley's Fantasy Take: If you looked at Chavis in 2019 and thought "I wish I could dial up the good *and* the bad by about 20 percent," Dalbec is the prospect for you. To be fair, I really never even thought he'd make it this far given the insane swing-and-miss. I'm still not convinced it's gonna work at the major league level, though. Dalbec should be owned in TDGX-sized leagues (~200 prospects rostered) because of his proximity and his crazy power upside. There's a chance you'll get a few "the good Mark Reynolds" years out of him. That being said, he's not gonna sniff my personal top-101.

4

Jarren Duran OF   OFP: 50   ETA: Late 2020
Born: 09/05/96   Age: 23   Bats: L   Throws: R   Height: 6'2"   Weight: 200
Origin: Round 7, 2018 Draft (#220 overall)

The Report: In a system that desperately needed a breakout prospect, Duran took the bull by the horns and ran with it. He obliterated High-A arms with his combination of a solid hitting approach and plus speed. At the plate Duran shows average bat speed with a smooth, line-drive stroke that he uses to shoot ball to all fields. While the home run power is well below average, he drives the gaps well, and his speed allows him to turn singles into doubles, and some doubles into triples. After playing second base in college and his first year in pro ball, Duran has transitioned well to center. His plus speed allows him to cover plenty of grass and he has a good first step and already has solid instincts. His arm is fringe-average, so while he can stand anywhere in the outfield, it only plays in left and center on an every day basis.

Variance: Medium. His first introduction to Double-A did not go smoothly, the power doesn't really play over-the-fence, and the bat could be knocked out of his hands against better arms. There is still a floor of a defensive contributor/pinch-runner even if the bat doesn't play at a high level.

Ben Carsley's Fantasy Take: Ah, now here's a guy I probably *am* too high on! I wish Duran had performed better once promoted to Portland, of course, but if you know anything about me, you know I fall head-over-heels for speedy hitters with contact skills. Sometimes that means I'm sitting alone in a dark room in a Jose Peraza shirsey (thanks, Bret), but other times it means I get in on the ground floor of your Ender Inciarte types. That's the dream for Duran–a dude who can fight his way to .280-plus averages with 30-plus steals without getting the bat knocked out of his hands. Given his proximity to the big leagues, he should be considered a top-150 fantasy prospect, even if there's more risk here than his High-A numbers would have you believe.

5. Thad Ward RHP   OFP: 50   ETA: 2021
Born: 01/16/97   Age: 23   Bats: R   Throws: R   Height: 6'3"   Weight: 182
Origin: Round 5, 2018 Draft (#160 overall)

The Report: The 2018 fifth-round choice enjoyed one of the more notable breakout campaigns of 2019, collecting 157 strikeouts in 126 1/3 innings between Low- and High-A. Ward's watershed year was aided by the addition of an 87-88 mph cutter that has plus, sharp horizontal action. He also employs a straight four-seamer and a two-seamer that has tail, both sitting between 92-95 mph.

Beyond the firm stuff, Ward also throws two breaking balls. His low-80s slider is a sweepy pitch with plus horizontal break and it's one of his swing-and-miss pitches, along with the cutter. He also throws an upper-70s, 12-6 curveball sparingly. Ward rounds out his deep arsenal with a high-80s sinking changeup that has late, hard downward action.

What makes this right-hander even more effective is his deceptive mechanics. Throwing from a three-quarters angle, Ward creates an unusual slot with his cross-fire delivery. This makes his cutter/slider combo even harder to hit. There is a lot to like in Ward's profile. But he has a long way to go, plus the possibility of becoming a reliever still lingers until he can prove his wiry frame can make it as a starter long-term.

Variance: High. We've seen a few college arms in the Red Sox system fizzle out after dominating the lower minors.

Ben Carsley's Fantasy Take: Two things can be true at once: Ward has dramatically increased in fantasy value since he was drafted, and Ward's fantasy value still isn't that high. If you're the type of masochist who plays in dynasty AL-only leagues or if your league rosters 300 prospects or something, then sure, Ward is worth buying. Otherwise, we're looking at a back-end starter or reliever in a system that's had quite a bit of trouble developing either. Barring another improvement that leads us to believe he's got a higher upside, Ward won't be fantasy-relevant until he's knocking on the door.

6 **Jay Groome   LHP**   OFP: 50   ETA: 2022
Born: 08/23/98   Age: 21   Bats: L   Throws: L   Height: 6'6"   Weight: 220
Origin: Round 1, 2016 Draft (#12 overall)

The Report: Groome did get back on the mound for few rehab outings coming off his Tommy John surgery last May. Fifteen months later, there are no real red flags. The fastball velocity isn't all the way back to his pre-surgery mid 90s, but he sits in the low 90s with some plane and arm-side wiggle. Unsurprisingly the fastball command isn't all there at present, but there's no obvious cause for concern long term, despite some effort and a bit of crossbody action to the delivery.

The curve still flashes at the top of the scale, but again, there are consistency issues with the pitch coming out of a long injury layoff. Groome threw his change a fair bit in the rehab outing I caught, but it's well below average. He struggled to turn it over, although it would flash fringe tumble. He's filled out some from his listed weight, maybe 20 or 30 pounds, but the build is more solid than soft, with a good, thick lower half. This ranking feels low, but there's enough uncertainty that it also might end up high. Groome has shown 70-grade stuff, and it's the body of a mid-rotation starter, but he has pitched fewer innings in four pro seasons than your average seventh-inning guy does in a year. Throw a dart.

Variance: Xtreme (which is higher than extreme). Groome has thrown 66 pro innings. He was drafted in 2016. There were some durability and command concerns before Tommy John. The stuff is already flashing back to where it was pre-surgery, but he's a long way away from the majors, and not much has gone right for him so far. That all said, if stuff starts going right, this OFP could get bumped up by midseason next year. There's also a chance he never pitches above Double-A. We told you it was xtreme.

Ben Carsley's Fantasy Take: Call me crazy, but until we have a better understanding of Song's military commitment and until Ward carries less reliever risk, I still think Groome is actually the best fantasy pitching prospect in this system. There's ridiculous risk in the profile, as mentioned above, but if it all clicks we're looking at a potential top-25 fantasy prospect and bona fide fantasy SP2. It also kind of feels like he'll emerge as a late-inning weapon for, like, the A's in 2024 at this point, so do with this type of variance what you will.

7 **Bryan Mata   RHP**   OFP: 50   ETA: Late 2020
Born: 05/03/99   Age: 21   Bats: R   Throws: R   Height: 6'3"   Weight: 160
Origin: International Free Agent, 2016

The Report: Mata cleaned up his control and command a bit in 2019, cutting his walk rate in half and making it to Double-A before he was old enough to hit up Cascade Barrel House. The fastball sits mid 90s, and is a bit of a bowling ball, but the offering plays down as Mata still isn't sure where it's going much of the time. After all, cutting his walk rate in half merely got the control to below-average, and the command a step below that. The slider is the best of the present secondaries, it can be a bit cutterish in the low 90s, but will flash razor blade action, and is the offspeed pitch most likely to end up above average. His curveball is a bit of an up-and-under thing from his lower slot, and on the short side, but every once in a while he will pop one to the backfoot of a lefty that makes you go, "hmm." The changeup lags behind the rest of the arsenal, lacking ideal velocity separation or much fade. The change and command issues may limit Mata to the pen, and neither of the breaking balls might end up good enough to make up for the command wobbles, further limiting him to middle relief. However, you don't have to squint too hard to see a good fastball/slider late inning arm. And there's a non-zero chance he sticks as a starter at least for a bit.

Variance: Medium. There's a lot of reliever risk, but I'm also willing to be patient with a 20-year-old who missed as many bats as he did in Double-A. There's enough feel for all three secondaries that you could bet on one or two of them getting to at least average—making Mata a low-end No. 3 or high-end No. 4 starter—but I wouldn't lay your mortgage payment on it.

Ben Carsley's Fantasy Take: It feels as though the general Prospect Industrial Complex has been praising Mata's stuff while lamenting his results for about four decades now. Mostly I just want him to exhaust his rookie eligibility so I can stop writing about him. You'll want to own him if he ends up closing, but if he doesn't, you … won't. Please continue to subscribe to Baseball Prospectus for our fantasy analysis.

8. Tanner Houck   RHP
OFP: 50   ETA: 2020 as needed
Born: 06/29/96   Age: 24   Bats: R   Throws: R   Height: 6'4"   Weight: 210
Origin: Round 1, 2017 Draft (#24 overall)

The Report: Houck finally made the transition to the bullpen in July, allowing him to lean heavily on his two best pitches. The fastball is a power two-seamer in the mid 90s with both sink and run and, when his command is right, it's very effective movement. He pairs it with a mid-80s slider that tunnels well off the fastball then makes a late, sharp left turn with good depth despite a low-three-quarters slot. It's a high-effort arm action, so the command can be a little loose on both offerings, and the changeup never really got there—hence the move to the pen—but Houck is a major-league ready pen arm with late-inning potential.

Variance: Low. Houck looks to be a reliever for the foreseeable future, but it's a plus/plus two-pitch mix, so that makes him a fairly safe bet to be a solid relief arm, command and control permitting.

Ben Carsley's Fantasy Take: The rare pitching prospect who I actually hope heads to the bullpen instead of sticking in the rotation, thereby enabling us to make "Houck: A ROOGY" jokes. Barring some injuries that lead to save changes, that figures to be about the extent of Houck's fantasy relevance as well.

9. Gilberto Jimenez OF
OFP: 50 **ETA:** 2023
Born: 07/08/00 Age: 19 Bats: B Throws: R Height: 5'11" Weight: 160
Origin: International Free Agent, 2017

The Report: An under-the-radar $10,000 IFA signing, Jimenez came stateside quickly and thrived during an aggressive 2019 assignment to the Penn League. The left-handed swing is ahead of the right-handed one at the moment, but even that is flat, contact-oriented and bordering on defensive or slappy at times. On better swings, you'd call Jimenez "effectively short to the ball," but he lacks present physicality, or much in the way of projection—he's athletic but a tad stocky. Power is never going to be a part of his game past legging out some extra bases on balls into the gaps. The right-handed swing is longer with more of a leg lift, but also with additional sync and timing issues. Jimenez is aggressive at the plate, but generally knows what he can get the barrel on, so there's the outline of an above-average hit tool here. I'd just like to see the swing get less slappy and to see him drive the ball against better velocity and location than he saw in the Penn League before I fully sign off.

I have no such quibbles with the footspeed. Jimenez is a plus-plus runner who posts above-average run times even when he's not even busting it. The speed plays down on the basepaths, as Jimenez's instincts are raw and he's hyper aggressive with his leads and baserunning. In the outfield, though, his instincts and footspeed give him plus range in center. He knows where to run to, can adjust his routes on the fly, and has the closing speed to get balls coming in or going out, gap to gap. Jimenez's arm strength is just average, but he gets throws out quickly and accurately.

Variance: High. Jimenez is a long way from the majors, and I'm not as convinced by the hit tool as the .360 batting average might make you think. The speed and glove give him a good base for some sort of major-league contribution, but that might end up being more extra outfielder.

Ben Carsley's Fantasy Take: A good one for your watch list, as he is very fast. A bad one to invest in heavily now, as he is very far away.

10. Matthew Lugo SS
OFP: 50 **ETA:** 2023
Born: 05/09/01 Age: 19 Bats: R Throws: R Height: 6'1" Weight: 185
Origin: Round 2, 2019 Draft (#69 overall)

The Report: The second of Boston's second-rounders in the 2019 draft, Lugo is a good projection bet, but pretty raw at present. He has a lithe, athletic frame that should grow into average power in his 20s and will flash some pop pull-side already from a bit of loft and above-average bat speed. Lugo can lack physicality at the plate, and the swing can get a little choppy against better velo. There's some natural inside-out when he's worked away, and he's quick inside if you try to bust him there. You don't have to squint too hard to see an average hit/power combo at maturity, although "maturity" is gonna be a long ways off. Lugo is an above-average runner, heady and aggressive on the basepaths. He can be a bit mechanical at shortstop at present, and I'm curious to see if some of the effort in the field gets smoothed out with more pro reps. The portrait of his future is more Monet than Courbet at present, but the upside is intriguing.

Variance: Very High. There's very little pro track record here and the overall profile is raw. Far from a lock to stick at shortstop or hit against better pitching.

Ben Carsley's Fantasy Take: Look, we all realize this isn't the most exciting system in the world, but I actually like Lugo as a flyer for those of you in super deep leagues despite his ranking here. For our purposes, better a good hitter who's not a lock to stick at short than a lock to stick at short who can't hit. Plus, what could go wrong when you bet on a Red Sox shortstop named Lugo?

The Next Ten

11 Ryan Zeferjahn RHP
Born: 02/28/98 Age: 22 Bats: R Throws: R Height: 6'5" Weight: 225
Origin: Round 3, 2019 Draft (#107 overall)

Zeferjahn was drafted in the third round by the Red Sox after three years of racking up strikeouts for the Jayhawks. He is a large human being, cutting a towering figure even while throwing a bullpen three hundred feet away. Once he's within 60 feet and six inches, you quickly figure out why he racked up plenty of walks as well. Although he gets over his lower half well, a twisting, torquey delivery with a long arm action negatively impacts his ability to throw strikes with his fastball or consistently start his slider in the zone. It's not traditional "tall pitcher problems," but results in the similar issues. The stuff may end up good enough to make the command a mere unfortunate footnote. The power fastball/slider combination got our attention in the Cape a couple summers ago, the heater still sits mid 90s, and the breaker still flashes plus-or-better. The Sox kept Zeferjahn somewhat stretched out in short-season ball, but given the present delivery issues, and a curve and change that lag behind the rest of the repertoire, he profiles best as a late inning reliever. However, he could be an impact pen arm quickly, as long as he can keep his Brooks Baseball page from looking like a Mondrian painting.

12 C.J. Chatham SS
Born: 12/22/94 Age: 25 Bats: R Throws: R Height: 6'3" Weight: 185
Origin: Round 2, 2016 Draft (#51 overall)

Chatham keeps hitting around .300 at every level, and that skill didn't fade for him this season in Double-A and a late-season Triple-A trial. As you'd expect, the former second-rounder has strong bat-to-ball ability and excellent barrel control in general; he can dunk singles about as well as any prospect this side of Nick Madrigal. He also plays a fine shortstop, with exposure to the other infield positions, and he's athletic in general. What he doesn't do is drive the ball for anything more than fringe gap power, and that limits the profile. We don't expect that to improve at this stage of the game for him, because his bat speed is limited. Overall, he projects to bring enough defensive versatility/value and hit tool to be a contributor in a utility or second-division role. He needs to keep hitting close to .300 to profile as a first-division starter, which is a tough ask given his lack of secondary offensive skills, but not impossible.

13 Durbin Feltman   RHP
Born: 04/18/97   Age: 23   Bats: R   Throws: R   Height: 6'0"   Weight: 205
Origin: Round 3, 2018 Draft (#100 overall)

When I saw Feltman in April for Portland, I really didn't expect him to remain list-eligible down here. He ranked fifth on this list last year, and he just looked far too good for the Eastern League. He was throwing 95 with movement — a few ticks down from where he'd been in college, but still impressive, and sometimes velocities aren't all the way there in the first couple weeks of the season. He mixed in a big, impressive sweeping slider. It had some slurviness too it, but not in a bad way. With Boston's bullpen woes, he looked like he'd be in the majors within months, if not weeks. Instead, Feltman struggled with walks at Double-A, and the fastball never truly came around. He didn't make it to Triple-A, let alone the majors. It's still impressive enough stuff to make this list, and he could still very easily be a late-innings arm soon. But his ranking speaks just as much to the weakness of the system depth as it does Feltman.

14 Antoni Flores   SS
Born: 10/14/00   Age: 19   Bats: R   Throws: R   Height: 6'1"   Weight: 190
Origin: International Free Agent, 2017

Flores did not perform nearly as well as Jimenez during the pair's aggressive Penn League assignments, but I wouldn't quibble too much with you if you thought the Venezuelan shortstop was the better long term performance bet. The bat is much rawer, but there's a potential average hit and power combo if Flores fills out and shortens up a little. He flashed some gap power and above-average bat speed early in the Penn League campaign, but the swing had gotten long and out of sync by the end of it, showing none of the bat control or pop he flashed in June. In the field, Flores is a pretty smooth shortstop, with enough arm for the six. His actions could be a little rough at times, but he's got a good shot to stick assuming he doesn't fill out too much more. The present frame reminds me a bit of a more physical Andrés Giménez at times. It's significantly less polish than Giménez though, and the bat is a huge risk until we see a more consistent swing and better performance stateside.

15 Nick Decker   OF
Born: 10/02/99   Age: 20   Bats: L   Throws: L   Height: 6'0"   Weight: 200
Origin: Round 2, 2018 Draft (#64 overall)

A year after being drafted in the second round, Decker still has some of the rawness you'd associate with a cold weather prep outfielder. But there is also some decent feel to hit here, and while the swing can wrap some and get long, he shows plus bat speed and above-average raw power as well. The defensive tools on the grass are all a bit fringy—especially for center—and his routes can be a bit ugly at times. Other days he'd look perfectly passable up-the-middle, but I expect he will fill out enough to force him to a corner regardless. The arm strength is fringe as well, so left is more likely than right, but most likely of all is a little bit of all three spots as a fourth outfielder with some pop. But keep an eye on how the bat develops here, because cold weather preps can also have slower development curves.

16 Jaxx Groshans   C
Born: 07/20/98   Age: 21   Bats: R   Throws: R   Height: 6'0"   Weight: 209
Origin: Round 5, 2019 Draft (#167 overall)

Groshans was divisive internally on the prospect team, and this is a bit of a compromise ranking. Evaluating college catchers post-draft is tricky. It's a long season and a lot of hours squatting behind the plate. Groshans is an athletic receiver, excellent moving laterally to block balls in the dirt, and flashes an easy plus arm. His frame is a bit on the slight side at present, reminding me some of Francisco Mejia's, so you will have to continue monitoring how the body holds up under a more rigorous pro workload behind the plate. The bat is decidedly not Mejia's, but Groshans is short to the ball, and will make hard, mostly line drive contact despite only average bat speed. There's a little loft in the swing too, so more power might come in the pros when he hasn't been catching for six straight months. You'd like to see him fill out a bit—he was relatively young for his draft class—and get that true fire hydrant catcher body, but I kind of like the Kevin Plawecki comp I heard put on him recently.

17 Cameron Cannon   IF
Born: 10/16/97   Age: 22   Bats: R   Throws: R   Height: 5'10"   Weight: 196
Origin: Round 2, 2019 Draft (#43 overall)

Cannon's swing and body type will remind you a bit of Colton Welker's. He presently lacks Welker's physicality and bat speed—although it's solid enough—but the approach is similar, swing hard with some loft and let God sort 'em out. He can make loud contact, but was vulnerable to pulling off offspeed moving down and/or away. He also doesn't have Welker's pro track record despite being almost exactly the same age. Cannon does have a chance to stick up the middle, although I suspect the foot speed and actions will limit him primarily to second base, but he'd likely be fine at third too. Ultimately Cannon will go as far as the bat takes him, and he'll need to adjust to offspeed stuff to get the most out of his swing, but a good bench infielder with plenty of doubles seems a plausible result.

18. Dedgar Jimenez   LHP
Born: 03/06/96   Age: 24   Bats: L   Throws: L   Height: 6'3"   Weight: 240
Origin: International Free Agent, 2012

I am a noted Dedgar enthusiast, and even I was surprised that Jeffrey asked me to write up Dedgar for this list, because I'm genuinely surprised that Dedgar made a list. Basically, imagine a burly lefty throwing a kitchen sink's worth of fringy-to-average stuff, with a low-90s fastball and a slider leading the way, and your mental image is probably about right on this one. He's really entertaining and fun to watch, but there's no projectability and he's not at all a typical top-20 system talent even given that he's still only 23. After 44 starts over three seasons in Double-A, the Red Sox gave Jimenez a shot in Triple-A in June, where he got shelled for two starts. He was demoted back and moved to the bullpen, where he pitched very well and soon picked up the closer's role. If this all sounds like he's going to be somewhere on the utility pitcher to LOOGY spectrum, well, he probably is. If this also sounds like we could've stopped writing about the system already as to not end up ranking members of the Future LOOGYs of Baseball, well, that's probably true too, but uniformity and all.

19. Yoan Aybar   LHP
Born: 07/03/97   Age: 22   Bats: L   Throws: L   Height: 6'3"   Weight: 165
Origin: International Free Agent, 2013

A former outfielder who could barely hit his weight, Aybar was transitioned to relief pitcher around the middle of 2018. And, in flashes, has shown why. The lefty sits 94-96 mph with 98 mph in his pocket when he needs it. He also offers an 84-87 mph wipeout slider with plus tilt, giving him a dominant fastball/slider combination. However, the reason why his 2019 ERA (4.61) looks the way it does is because of major control issues, as he walked 41 batters over 56 2/3 innings. That said, he also struck out 70. His delivery and electric arsenal remind me of Aroldis Chapman, with his high leg kick towards the stomach with similar arm motion and release point. But repeating his delivery and release point are a concern. His athleticism on the mound gives me hope he can harness those issues and alleviate his high walk rate.

20. Aldo Ramirez   RHP
Born: 05/06/01   Age: 19   Bats: R   Throws: R   Height: 6'0"   Weight: 180
Origin: International Free Agent, 2018

Ramirez is an undersized Mexican righty who signed late and lacks much physical projection, but showed feel for pitching far beyond what you'd expect from functionally a high school senior. The fastball sat in the low 90s for the most part, although he could ramp it into an average velocity band in the early innings. Ramirez can struggle to locate the fastball arm-side due to some natural cut and crossfire in his delivery, but the velocity comes relatively easily. The curveball is very projectable, mid-70s with good shape and command at present, although he doesn't always get tight, late break with it. He's confident enough to throw it early in counts, when he's behind, or in jams. Ramirez can manipulate it for strikes or to chase, and it's advanced feel for spin, even if the pitch only projects as average. The change is firm, without ideal velocity separation, but he'll flash some some decent circle action when he can keep the cambio around 85. It's well behind the curve at present, but also projectable. The overall package here is three potential average offerings, but there's a long way to get there, and the more likely outcome is an up-and-down swing/middle reliever type. Still, Ramirez is definitely worth a follow as he heads to full-season ball next year.

Personal Cheeseball

PC **Jenrry Mejia   RHP**
Born: 10/11/89   Age: 30   Bats: R   Throws: R   Height: 6'0"   Weight: 205
Origin: International Free Agent, 2007

I passed the New Jersey bar exam in July 2013. It was the culmination of a winding path towards being an attorney that saw me go to law school and then decide not to practice and then change my mind a few years later and decide to take the exam. (Aspiring attorneys, I don't recommend having to relearn all of law school three years later.)

Anyways, Jenrry Mejia started for the Mets in Miami on the night in between the MBE and the essays. I watched the game while trying with mixed success to control terrible anxiety, and I have memories of him pitching very well. Looking it up, these are apparently the lies your brain tells you six-and-a-half years later. It was the start before the one during my bar exam where he came up off Tommy John surgery and pitched seven shutout innings. In the start I remember from that night he actually gave up three runs over six and was tagged with the loss.

It's been an up and down journey for both of us. My time practising wasn't any kind of success; I hated doing bankruptcy and foreclosure work, which was the best job I could find at the time, and ended up back in my previous real-world profession within a year. I consider everything in that period in my life to have ended up being really expensive training for being a baseball writer.

Mejia's career would be on a rollercoaster too. His starting pitching promise never panned out, whether due to lack of durability or mishandling by the Mets or something else. He'd eventually land as the team's closer, and held that role for much of the 2014 season. Warming up for his first save in 2015, he tweaked his elbow, and shortly thereafter, he was suspended for the first time for PEDs. He failed twice more for steroids over the next year, and ended up permanently banned from MLB.

After some wild accusations against Major League Baseball, he'd fade into the background, popping up every offseason for unaffiliated winter ball and the annual oddity of agreeing to a Mets contract that he couldn't fulfill. He was quietly reinstated with conditions attached late in 2018, and the Red Sox signed him to a minor-league deal before 2019. He didn't pitch well in the minors, but he did pitch most of the season, and he's back down pitching for Toros del Este in the Dominican at press time. And I'll always remember him for being the guy on the mound when I had to control a panic attack during the bar exam, and root for him to make it back, which is about as cheesy as it gets.

Low Minors Sleeper

LMS

Brendan Cellucci   RHP
Born: 06/30/98   Age: 22   Bats: L   Throws: L   Height: 6'4"   Weight: 201
Origin: Round 12, 2019 Draft (#377 overall)

Well we have already put a bunch of Boston's 2019 draft on this list so let's continue. I considered Chris Murphy—their sixth-round pick—for this spot. He's your standard fifth starter type with below-average fastball velo and three polished secondary options, with one or two that might bump average, but let's go with the lefty power arm instead. Cellucci got $345k as a 12th-round draft-eligible sophomore, because you don't find too many southpaws that touch 96 with a potential plus slider on Day Three. The curve might end up above-average as well, while the command and change are existent, but will limit him to the reliever-only track. He could be a fast mover on the strength of his top two pitches though, and adds another intriguing relief option to the Red Sox system. Normally we wouldn't call relief prospects "intriguing" as a rule, but then again did you watch the 2019 Boston bullpen?

Top Talents 25 and Under (as of 4/1/2020)

1. Rafael Devers
2. Andrew Benintendi
3. Michael Chavis
4. Triston Casas
5. Noah Song
6. Bobby Dalbec
7. Jarren Duran
8. Darwinzon Hernandez
9. Thad Ward
10. Jay Groome

The Red Sox apologist's take is that "25 and Under" is an arbitrary designation. Were this, say a "27 and under" list, we could include Mookie Betts, Xander Bogaerts, and Eduardo Rodriguez, and we'd feel much better about the depth of this group. In fact, it'd still be in the running for one of the best such collections of talent in the game. Yes, Boston's farm system has been terrible for a few seasons now, but that's in part because it had graduated a tremendous amount of young talent. Any budding narrative that the Sox will be unable to compete because of their desolate farm–that new "Chief Baseball Officer" Chaim Bloom needs to rebuild this talent base from scratch–willfully overlooks that a whole lot of Boston's best players are under 30.

And yet, a consequence of Boston's offensive core being so good while so young is that they're getting very expensive as they peak. Betts, as you may have heard, is entering his walk year. So too is Jackie Bradley, Jr. Bogaerts signed a six-year, $120 million deal that, while perhaps a bargain compared to what similar talents make, still pays him $20 million a year. E-Rod is entering his second arbitration year. Benintendi is now arbitration-eligible. When those players were all making, like, $30 million combined, it was easy to support them with megastars like Chris Sale, J.D. Martinez, and David Price. Now that the members of the young core are being paid as stars themselves, the Red Sox are going to need to supplement them with new homegrown talent.

That might be a problem, because aside from Devers and Benintendi, their 25U list ain't so hot.

We'll start with the good news. Devers took the much anticipated leap in 2019, emerging as one of the best young hitters in the game and improving his defense at third. He finished 11th in all of baseball in BWARP. He's only just turned 23. He's an absolute stud, and should bat in the middle of Boston's lineup for the next half-decade.

While Devers got much, much better in 2019, Benintendi got worse. His slugging percentage declined despite the hitter-friendly balls. His average dropped despite a career-best BABIP. He walked less, struck out more, and even had a rough season in left field, per FRAA. Everything about Benny's past performance and overall profile suggests this was more a bump in the road than a sign of anything of lasting regression, but still it is, to use a scouting term, not what you want.

The final two non-prospect members of the 25U list, Chavis and Hernandez, have not yet convincingly displayed that they deserve prominent roles on first-division clubs, though it's clear they belong in some capacity. After setting the world on fire in his first six weeks in the majors, Chavis struggled badly, striking out a ton as pitchers exploited the hole in his swing. He has power, can capably man either spot on the left side of the infield, and is adorably enthusiastic, but we still don't know if he'll make enough contact to play every day. Hernandez was often dominant when on the mound, but also issued more walks than Rover and he dispelled any notion that he can start. He's so talented that there's a chance he's Josh Hader-lite, but he's so wild that there's also a chance he's, like, a left-handed Tayron Guerrero.

That's where the Red Sox are with their truly young talent, then: a group that includes one of the game's best players, a role-6 outfielder coming off a down year, two wild-cards and then the top-six members of a bottom-five system. It's a collection of talent that's a long ways away from the terrible Angels 25U lists of a few seasons ago, but perhaps even farther away from a time when Boston's young core was considered the envy of the league.

Odds are one of Bloom's chief directives is to improve the young talent in Boston's organization. The real question is: can he do so without dramatically lowering his current squad's ceiling?

Part 3: Featured Articles

The Baseball Is Juiced (Again)

Robert Arthur

This article originally appeared at Baseball Prospectus on April 5, 2019.

It started when the normally reliable Chris Sale got lit up for three homers by the Mariners in the Red Sox's season opener. It was part of a record number of taters that flew on Opening Day, as starters from Sale to Zack Greinke were taken deep by the handful. Then Christian Yelich hit a home run in each of his first four games, tying yet another MLB record, this one for consecutive games with a dinger to start a season.

It didn't take long for fans and players to begin whispering and tweeting about the baseballs being juiced again. It's early yet for us to come to any definitive conclusion about the 2019 season, but preliminary data shows that the baseball has returned to its aerodynamic peak. Whether that means this season will smash home run records like 2017 did remains to be seen.

Before home run explosion over the last few years, no one worried too much about the baseball's air resistance. While MLB and Rawlings (the company that manufactures the official baseballs) kept track of dozens of metrics to make sure that the ball was consistent from month to month, they didn't measure drag.

But drag is incredibly important in determining how likely a hitter is to knock one out of the park. As baseballs become more aerodynamic, they travel further given a certain initial velocity. A deep fly ball that might have been caught at the warning track can instead go into the first row of the stands. A three percent change in drag coefficient can work to add about five feet to a well-hit fly ball, which can in turn increase home runs league wide by an astounding 10-15 percent.

It's possible to measure the aerodynamics of the baseball using the pitch-tracking radars currently in place in each MLB ballpark. By calculating the loss of speed from when the pitch is released to when it crosses the plate, you can directly measure the drag coefficient on the baseball. I first wrote about the role of decreasing drag in boosting home runs in 2017, and MLB's commission of scientists and statisticians later confirmed that the more aerodynamic baseballs in use that year were largely to blame for the spike in home runs. The same commission rejected some alternate hypotheses, like rising temperatures and a league-wide boost in launch angle pushing more balls over the fence.

The current era has featured some large fluctuations in drag coefficient, leading to first an explosion in 2016 and 2017, and then a dialing back of homers last year. Curious about the record-breaking home run tallies in the last few days, I used the same methodology to measure the aerodynamics of the baseballs so far in 2019.

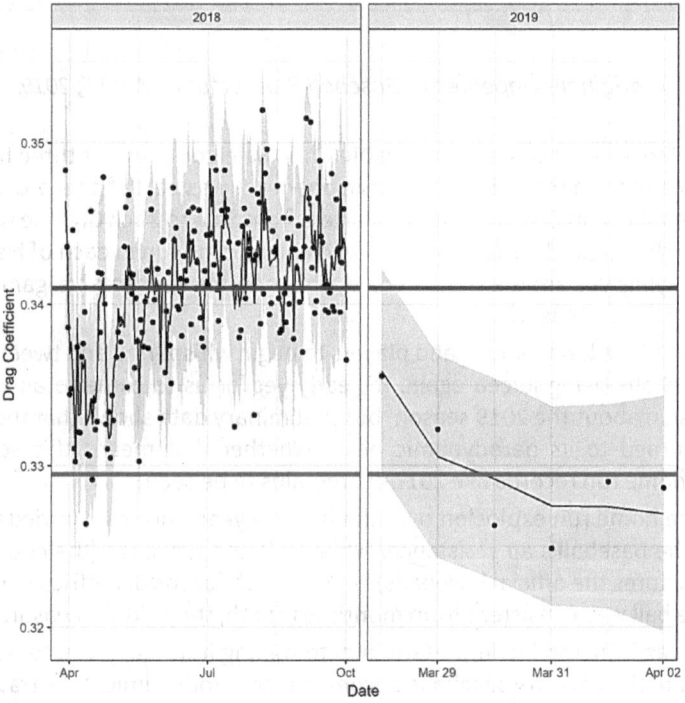

We're only a week into the 2019 season, but the drag numbers so far are among the lowest recorded in the last calendar year. With apologies for gory math, the current 2019 season average drag coefficient (the red line) would be below the 95 percent credible interval (the shaded area) for about nine-tenths of the 2018 season. (I used a Bayesian Random Walk model implemented in INLA to calculate these credible intervals, averaging the drag numbers in each game and adjusting for park.)

There were only a handful of six-day stretches in 2018 that had drag numbers below what we're seeing now, and most were in late June and early July. All of this means that 2019's data so far is quite a bit different than what we saw through most of last year.

These drag coefficients factor out the effects of temperature and air density, so they aren't a product of April cold. However, the numbers could be deceptive if the radars used to track pitches have changed from year to year. I consulted with some experts within baseball who were not aware of any specific modifications to the radar this year that could produce this pattern, but it's an important caveat of which to be aware.

On the one hand, it's only been six days, and we don't quite have the statistical basis to say that these drag coefficients are unprecedented compared to 2018. On the other hand, we've witnessed about 5,000 fastballs so far this season, so it's not as if our sample size is small. At least so far, the baseball has played like it's much more aerodynamic than it was last year. In fact, the current drag coefficient is really only comparable to 2017, when the baseballs were more aerodynamic than they had been in at least a decade.

It's not just fancy radar tracking indicating that the baseball is flying through the air more easily. The current number of home runs per game (as of this writing) is the highest it's been since the heady days of 2017, the year that teams and players broke dinger-related records everywhere you looked. That's especially remarkable considering that we're in what is typically the coldest part of the regular season, when lower temperatures and higher winds tend to suppress offense and keep balls in the air within the park. Comparing only from April to April, this year's rate of home runs per fly ball is even a little bit higher than it was in 2017.

With that said, the current measurements are no guarantee that 2019 will be another year of record-shattering homer hitting. The trouble with the drag measurements is that they are not consistent from June to August, from week to week, or even sometimes from day to day. Whether because of natural manufacturing variation or differences in the underlying supplies of cowhide and thread that go into the baseballs, drag has a tendency to fluctuate up and down over the course of a year. So the homers that fly in the first week of April wouldn't necessarily clear the fence a week later.

It's possible that this one-week drop in drag coefficient subsides and the baseball returns to its 2018 levels. On the other hand, it's almost equally probable that the ball becomes even more slippery and flies ever farther. Either way, it's clear that the baseball's air resistance is something to keep an eye on for the remainder of the 2019 season.

—*Robert Arthur is an author of Baseball Prospectus.*

The Moral Hazard of Playing It Safe

Craig Goldstein

This article originally appeared at Baseball Prospectus on August 6, 2019.

A couple days prior to the trade deadline, amidst a sea of tranquility posing as the lead up to the trade deadline, Bob Nightengale took to Twitter. Nightengale, who was probably wearing his pants backwards at the time, tweeted that MLB GMs were coming around on the idea that the unified trade deadline should be moved back from July 31 to August 15, so they could better assess their positions in the standings and whether they should buy or sell. To which I said:

This might strike some as reductive and churlish. And it might be that, but it isn't really wrong, either. Jeff Quinton wrote a great piece discussing the environmental factors that enable front offices to avoid risk without upsetting the apple cart within their own fanbases. I don't believe that it goes far enough, however. His article gives us the proper framework through which to understand why these behaviors have been allowed to seep into front offices throughout the league. Understanding the reasons behind these actions are different from excusing them, though, and GMs should not be let off the hook for their non-competitive approach to the trade deadline (much less the offseason).

⚾   ⚾   ⚾

It's fair to say that fans as a group have rarely, if ever, been pro-player. It is also fair to say that in the time during and following the Moneyball revolution, the pendulum swung from fans who cared intensely about winning in the moment (and thus might be intolerant of a rebuilding approach) to fans who supported building a team that could compete throughout multiple seasons, viewing the playoffs as a crapshoot, with the thought that getting multiple bites at the apple was a better approach than taking a bigger bite in any one season.

There's nothing wrong with that approach, and I still find merit in that argument. However, it seems that the pendulum has swung too far in that direction. Teams are overvaluing some of the individual factors that make themselves long-term contenders rather than attempting to seize a championship when given the opportunity. It's a difficult needle to thread.

And surely, they (and those in similar positions) would have liked another two weeks to clarify where they stand so as to better marshal their resources. We've all asked for a few more minutes when staring at a menu. But all of these GMs and front office personnel are where they are to make difficult decisions. They have proprietary data and internal analysts dedicated to understanding their position relative to the rest of the league, and how any move in the here and now impacts their long-term vision. To complain (if that report is accurate) that over half the season is not enough to properly assess their season is bullshit of the highest order. Move the deadline, and you'd simply have increasingly discounted trade offers because teams would be acquiring even less control of anyone they're acquiring, rental or not.

Major league front offices are behaving like the managers they lampooned two decades ago. They're effectively sacrificing a runner to second in the ninth inning—not because it's the correct move, but rather because it is safe. It used to be that the phrase "moral hazard" was used to describe general managers who made ill-fated, short-sighted decisions aimed at locking in wins and securing their jobs at the expense of their team's future. Now, general managers are guilty of committing moral hazards in the opposite direction, playing it utterly safe and terrified of becoming scapegoats.

In lieu of bold action, they opt to pussyfoot around a current window of contention, choosing instead to play the long game and stack up years of control like they're blocks in a game of Jenga. GMs pass on signing quality players in free agency because the back-end of the deal might look bad, and because they might be able to squeeze out 70 percent of the production from a player who costs a tenth as much. That's a safer investment, too, because it's also hard to prove a negative—it's impossible to prove that Manny Machado would make the Mets a playoff team in 2019-2020, but it's easy to say that the back half of Robinson Cano's contract sucks. Owners, who rule over GM's jobs, are also humans with human brain processes that will always make the so-called albatross contract uglier than the road not taken.

These days, GMs are remembered for the bad deals they make and the surplus value they generate, not the acquisition of expensive, necessary talents that meet their market worth (or fall slightly short while still providing significant on-field value). And front offices know that one or two expensive misfires can cost them their jobs, no matter how many good deals they make.

No front office exemplifies this ethos more than the Toronto Blue Jays. General Manager Ross Atkins had this to say following the Blue Jays underwhelming trade deadline:

This is by no means the first time that an executive will cite years of control to justify their actions, which is often just another way of saying "don't look at what we got, look at how much we got of it." Atkins touts quantity to elide the discussion of quality—either, that of the players acquired, or those given up. Remember: the other teams presumably value years of control, too.

Atkins also had some thoughts to offer regarding free agents back in early 2018:

This ignores, of course, whether the player can create enough value in the front end of a contract to justify the longer term of a deal, and the decline that often occurs in the back end. It also ignores whether the player can fill a need the team requires and put them in a position to compete for and win a championship. But as teams seemingly avoid contention at all, where they might end up having to consider and later justify some of these tough decisions, we still see risk-averse approaches.

Anthony Fenech's article on two trades that recently extended GM Al Avila didn't make got at this issue rather well:

> Passing on those deals was defensible: Both players had yet to break out and trading [Michael] Fulmer—a pitcher who appeared to be a future ace, no matter his injury concerns—would have taken serious gumption, opening Avila up to strong criticism.

Avoiding strong criticism is something each of us can understand as a motivation, but the avoidance of criticism only matters if that criticism is valid. In Fulmer's case, shoving his injury concerns aside affects not only the years that the team controls him (he is currently missing a full season due to Tommy John surgery) but also the quality of those seasons, as his knee and elbow injuries combined to dampen his effectiveness even when healthy enough to pitch. But it was easy to present the then-current image of Fulmer as a top of the rotation pitcher who the team had under its domain for the next five seasons as something to build around. The status quo isn't nearly as often second-guessed as a decision that disrupts it.

⚾ ⚾ ⚾

MLB GMs are risk-averse to a fault. They are ivy-educated and consulting firm-approved, and yet they can't seem to avoid leaving wins on the table in their all-consuming lust for a non-existent $/WAR championship. They are supposed to zig when everyone else zags, and not merely pay lip service to the idea of zigging through a calculated PR plan built on convincing the fan base their approach is novel when it actually apes most of their competitors. Instead they've become far more concerned with making safe, accepted-by-the-new-common-wisdom decisions, such that our prior understanding of what a moral hazard is has become inverted.

I can't blame them entirely, and not only because of the reasons that Quinton illuminated in his article, but also because of the damage wrought by the introduction of the second wild card (WC2) spot. MLB's desire to have more teams in playoff contention has sparked anti-competitive behavior. Teams know now that they do not need to swing big as they assemble their roster because there is a good chance that a mediocre team can either catch fire and capture a division, or muddle along until they back into the WC2.

Simultaneously, the one-game playoff has neutered the WC1, putting an entire season on the flip of a coin like some sort of baseball-obsessed Anton Chigurh. While the one-game playoff makes sense as a way to increase the value of winning a division, it also means that if a front office doesn't like its chances of overcoming a behemoth like the Dodgers or Astros in the offseason, they have few incentives to chase glory. Similarly, the relative inaction in the NL Central at the trade deadline—despite a wide open division—can be explained by the idea that any high-variance investment could still result in only a wild card (or worse) result, given the mere two months left in the season to make an impact.

⚾ ⚾ ⚾

As stated at the top, we should not confuse reasons for excuses. The implementation of the second wild card is just one of many environmental factors that influence how each front office operates. I am convinced that it is one of the larger factors, but I am also convinced that organizations need to shed the yoke of "efficiency at all costs" so that they can instead pursue competition, as the spirit of the game intends. Until they do, we're all deadline losers.

—*Craig Goldstein is an author of Baseball Prospectus.*

Index of Names

Arauz, Jonathan 102
Aybar, Yoan 104, 117
Barnes, Matt 53
Benintendi, Andrew 22
Bogaerts, Xander 24
Bradley Jr., Jackie 87
Brasier, Ryan 55
Brewer, Colten 57
Brice, Austin 59
Cannon, Cameron 88, 116
Casas, Triston 89, 107
Cashner, Andrew 61
Castillo, Rusney 102
Cellucci, Brendan 119
Centeno, Juan 102
Chatham, C.J. 102, 114
Chavis, Michael 26
Dalbec, Bobby 90, 108
Decker, Nick 102, 115
Devers, Rafael 28
Diaz, Danny 102
Downs, Jeter 91
Duran, Jarren 92, 109
Eovaldi, Nathan 63
Esplin, Tyler 102
Feltman, Durbin 96, 115
Flores, Antoni 102, 115
Groome, Jay 97, 111
Groshans, Jaxx 116
Hart, Kyle 104
Hembree, Heath 65
Hernandez, Darwinzon 67
Hernandez, Gorkys 102
Hernández, Marco 31
Holt, Brock 33
Houck, Tanner 98, 112
Howlett, Brandon 102
Jimenez, Dedgar 117
Jimenez, Gilberto 93, 113
Johnson, Brian 104
Lakins, Travis 104
Lin, Tzu-Wei 102
Longhi, Nick 102
Lucroy, Jonathan 35
Lugo, Matthew 102, 113
Martinez, J.D. 37
Mata, Bryan 99, 111
Mazza, Chris 104
Mejia, Jenrry 104, 118
Moreland, Mitch 39
Murphy, Chris 104
Nunez, Jhon 102
Ockimey, Josh 102
Osich, Josh 69
Pearce, Steve 41
Pedroia, Dustin 94
Peraza, José 43
Pérez, Martín 71
Pillar, Kevin 45
Plawecki, Kevin 47
Poyner, Bobby 104
Ramirez, Aldo 104, 117

Ramirez, Erasmo 104
Rei, Austin 102
Reyes, Denyi 104
Rodriguez, Eduardo 73
Sale, Chris 75
Shawaryn, Michael 104
Song, Noah 100, 108
Taylor, Josh 77
Vázquez, Christian 51
Velázquez, Hector 79
Verdugo, Alex 49
Walden, Marcus 81
Ward, Thad 101, 110
Weber, Ryan 104
Wilson, Marcus 102
Wong, Connor 95
Workman, Brandon 83
Wright, Steven 85
Zeferjahn, Ryan 104, 114